The Littlest Crusade

Copyright © Desmond Long, 2013. All rights reserved. No part of this book may be reproduced or transmitted in any form or by any means, electronic or mechanical, including photocopying, recording, or by any information storage and retrieval system, without permission in writing from the publisher.

First edition 2012 published by Millennial Mind Publishing,
an imprint of American Book Publishing.

Second edition 2013 published by Desmond Long.
Enquiries: www.thelittlestcrusade.com
Orders: www.thelittlestcrusade.com, www.amazon.co.uk, www.amazon.com

Author blog: www.thelittlestcrusade.com/blog

The Littlest Crusade

Cover designed by Akira (http:// www.ebook-cover-design.com)

The author/publisher specifically disclaims any responsibility for any liability, loss, or risk, personal or otherwise, which is incurred as a consequence, directly or indirectly, of the use and application of any of the contents of this book. In such situations where medical, legal, or other professional services may apply, please seek the advice of such professionals directly.

ISBN: 978-0-473-26640-0

The Littlest Crusade

By Desmond Long

*To everything there is a season,
and a time to every purpose
Ecclesiastes 3:1*

This book is dedicated to me,
because that's all there is.

Foreword

As the discoverer and developer of Induced After Death Communication (IADC), and as a researcher of Near Death Experiences (NDEs) and After Death Communication (ADC) for many years, I have to admit that I was somewhat startled when I encountered the work of Desmond Long.

Mr. Long has an unquestionably unique story. Although it is not inconsistent with the thousands of accounts I have heard from people who have come close to death or have experienced a loving encounter with a deceased loved one, nevertheless Des has ventured beyond that into a completely unexplored landscape. Dwelling in the remote and sparsely populated islands of New Zealand in the South Pacific, he used a personal variation of IADC to follow his wife Val within a week of her death. He reportedly visited every few days for eight months.

What did he encounter? The noted British scientist Sir James Jeans stated that the more he studied the universe, the less it appeared like a giant machine and the more like a great thought. Einstein suggested that material form is an illusion or construction of the human mind, a pattern we put together in order to relate to it. In his own excursion Des invites us to look at the universe and who we are with completely new eyes.

As a psychologist with a background in research, and as the Director of the Center for Grief and Traumatic Loss, LLC in Libertyville, Illinois, I am less interested in philosophical, esoteric or theological viewpoints than I am with helping people who suffer profoundly.

Nevertheless we are surrounded by mysteries and challenges. They are part of the human condition. The Littlest Crusade examines in intricate detail some of the most compelling questions relating to our existence. Des takes afterlife communication to places it has never been before.

Desmond Long's account is variously beautiful and appalling, and he is well placed to provide it. As a clinician he has specialized for 20 years in a raft of trance techniques as well as Eye Movement Desensitization and Reprocessing (EMDR), to meet the therapeutic needs of his clients. His interpretation and personal use of a variation of IADC is intriguing, and his conclusions are no less than mind boggling.

Allan L. Botkin, Psy. D.
Induced After Death Communication:
A New Therapy for Healing Grief and Trauma

Preface

In the late 1990s psychologists in the United States discovered the means to manipulate the human brain so that the average man or woman was able to communicate with people who had passed on. Duplicated research proved this. Its reality could not be seriously questioned. Something became possible that was not possible in the past!

In 2007, within days of my wife dying, I used this modality to catch up with her and share her sometimes troubled journey from the deathbed to vistas unfolding before her and beyond. To the best of my knowledge, never before has a scientifically-validated excursion been undertaken into the after-death state, in a protracted and detailed manner.

I was shocked by the clarity of what overtook me, the extent to which my most probing questions were answered, and the depth of detail that was explained. Most of this did not come from my wife, Val, but from others in her surroundings who used the opportunity to convey a broad range of information, perspectives and advice from one plane of existence to another.

What sort of information? A picture was presented that I had never read or heard about. Nothing I was able to relate to seemed off limits.

At my prompting the following and other subjects were discussed:

The unborn baby who dies.
Death, exactly what is it?
The famous Kennedy family.
What is prophecy all about?
Is abortion right or wrong?
Does God answer prayers?
What is physical life for?
Jesus and Hitler, what are we to make of them, and what is their relationship?
Just what is humanity?
The ultimate destiny of every human being.
What is going wrong with the planet and its inhabitants?
The mysterious subconscious mind.
The demise of the Christian Church.
The Antichrist and demons.
What are we to make of so-called aliens?
Why does illness occur?
Is euthanasia right or wrong?
Mother Teresa and her betrayal by God.
Past lives, fact or fiction?
Heaven and hell.
The Second Coming of Jesus Christ.
Where does this account take us and what does it seek to achieve?

What I was told is quite foreign to the generally accepted and most cherished concepts of a Christian society, appallingly so. I will be searching in the light of what I encountered for the rest of my life. Perhaps you will as well.

It starts in the grim hospital room where my wife spent her final days, a situation which to me symbolized the substance and reality of the physical journey. It then moves beyond this iron embrace to an aspect of consciousness existing between physical life and the dimensions of spirit, somewhat to my dismay.

The journey continues as a meandering tour within a strange world where the mundane and the profound are examined. This unfolds to reveal the dawning potential and destiny of every human being.

Where there is light there is usually darkness to be found. The Beings who guided this excursion took the opportunity to broadcast a statement. This book is the statement. I am only the postman, the one who delivers the message.

Dates attached to the spirit communications are not always in chronological sequence, as preference has been given to an orderly development of the subjects.

Chillingly, it is both an ultimatum and a plea. There was always going to exist a time when the communities of the developed world achieved the maturity and ability to respond to the challenges we face on a global scale. *The time is now.* In these pages you are advised of your responsibilities and the consequences of failing to act. With natural law there is no punishment. There is merely the implacable influence of cause and effect. Learning will proceed as always. How it does is up to you. No longer is it possible to say you don't know.

Table of Contents

Foreword 9
Preface 11
I. Goodbye Val 17
II. The Early Days 27
III. Moving Away 43
IV. Tanya 49
V. Animals in Spirit 63
VI. Defining a Spirit 71
VII. The Journey of a Dead Baby 89
VIII. Does a Spirit Even Exist? 97
IX. Many Mysteries 107
X. Personalities in Spirit 115
XI. Jesus and Hitler: Their Relationship 123
XII. Looking at the Face of God 133
XIII. Different Explanations: Why? 139

XIV. The Late Great Human Race 151
XV. A Land of Suffering: The Physical 157
XVI. Prophecy in Detail 163
XVII. The Prophets Who Guide Us.................................171
XVIII. Death Throes of Christianity?..............................177
XIX. Heaven and Hell 183
XX. The Second Coming of Jesus Christ 189
XXI. The Book's Dedication..193
XXII Questions and Answers 195
Epilogue 239
Acknowledgements...241
About the Author 243

I. Goodbye Val

Never had I seen a person look like that. As I entered the hospital ward, my wife of nearly forty years was sitting bolt upright in bed, supported by pillows. Her head was immobile but her eyes were frantic and darting like those of a trapped rat. Her tongue protruded from her mouth and her lips hung loosely. Obviously, she had suffered another stroke.

For three years Val had been a tetraplegic, able to move only her eyes and one hand, which hovered next to her face like a misshapen claw. For three years she spent much of her time weeping bitterly or mired in lethargy. Her voice was a hoarse whisper, painstakingly squeezed out. For three years she croaked a desperate message to me, "Take me home, please take me home."

For three years I refused.

During most of that time home was a forty-five minute drive north on New Zealand's Kapiti Coast. Val lived in Emmerson House, a small hospital unit in Porirua, reserved for the profoundly disabled. She hated it. She feared it, despite its competent and caring personnel. I visited her every second day, to feed her the evening meal as we had once taken turns to spoon feed our two babies.

That day, sitting bolt upright in a Wellington Hospital bed, Val was being fed through an intravenous tube. I moved closer and touched her arm. She didn't seem to notice. Her eyes were panic-stricken and flicking around the room. Abruptly she hunched into convulsions, and blood trickled from her mouth onto a towel.

I went to the nursing station and explained that my wife had not sat upright for three years. She was unable to tolerate the posture for more than three hours, even tied into a wheelchair.

"Why not?"

"It was the pain. She would cry out and beg to go back to bed."

The nurse, supportive and pleasant though she was, explained that Val would choke if she were to lie down. The registrar would be there later in the day, and there were only two doctors for three wards, one of which was a birthing unit.

"What medication is Val on?"

Again referring to notes, the nurse explained, "Painkillers would lower Val's blood pressure to a dangerous level. The intravenous antibiotics she was on have been discontinued. She is on no medication." I was feeling too punch-drunk to get angry. "Yes," the nurse continued, "Val did suffer another stroke. Clearly, death is imminent, but mainly as a result of septicemia." I already knew her digestive system had broken down, swamping her body with poison. Then there was the long term multiple sclerosis.

I put spoonfuls of sugar into my coffee and stirred. The cafeteria on the ground floor contained half a dozen people, most of them hospital staff.

At least they could give Val some painkillers! How long had she been propped upright before I arrived? It was a wonder she could breathe. Perhaps if she were able to scream they would have provided painkillers or turned her on her side so she could lie down without choking on her tongue or getting blood in her lungs.

The coffee seemed cold, so I put in more sugar.

Val and I probably were an unusual couple. From the time she was a preschooler she was able to see spirits, dead people, and talk with them. It just happened. She accepted it.

It was the same with me. I had an unremarkable, if somewhat skewed, childhood. As a preschooler during the years of the Second World War, I rarely encountered my father, Lance. He served in the Air Force with the Americans in the Pacific campaign, in Guadalcanal, Bougainville, Green Island and other parts of the Solomons.

My mother Irene and I lived in the tiny village of Murchison, isolated in the northern reaches of the Southern Alps in New Zealand. I was the oldest child in the entire generation. As a young woman Mum suffered from a social phobia and was profoundly shy and non-communicative. She rarely spoke, even to me. My mother kept completely to herself, isolated from the neighbors. I did not play with other children. There was just Mum and me.

When I was three years old, an event took place that changed my life in a matter of minutes.

My mother and I were walking by the Matakitaki River not far from our house in Hotham Street. I slipped down the bank into the river and was carried downstream into the local swimming hole. One of the youngsters there saw what was happening, rescued me, and deposited my semi-conscious form on the bank at my mother's feet.

There I lay, panicking and choking, as Mum watched, paralyzed with horror and shock. The rescuer turned me onto my stomach and drained the water from my lungs.

I felt terribly betrayed. My mother was supposed to look after me. She was the only person with whom I felt safe, yet she let this happen. She watched me continue to die and did not help in my rescue.

It was the ultimate rejection and hurt even more than the terrible pain of drowning. It was so painful that it took me years to feel safe enough to get close to another person. Val was the only one I trusted enough to let my defenses down.

It was decades after the trauma in Murchison, while in a hypnotherapeutic trance, that I recalled what took place during those seminal minutes.

When Dad came home in 1945 nothing much changed. My father was almost as withdrawn as Mum. My parents seldom spoke so I remained in a cocoon of isolation. When I started school I was barely able to speak, and considered retarded.

There was an upside, though. During my preschool years the silence was broken by spirit, with whom I became more comfortable than with anyone in physical. Not that they spoke to me at the time, but at least they talked, and I listened. Later they included me and eventually became an important part of my life.

Val's childhood in Wellington was quite different. As the years went by, her parents grew apart and their relationship bitter. Val took her mother's side and eventually became emotionally remote from her father.

During our married life she continued this habit of protection by ring-fencing herself from men. She created an emotional distance, pushed me away, and identified me as the enemy. This impacted on our relationship, especially as multiple sclerosis froze her body and tightened its grip on her mind.

As fate would have it, this tendency of Val's to identify me as the enemy and reject me, treat me as once her mother treated her father, resurrected the awful betrayal the preschool child perceived at the hands of his mother while he lay dying on the riverbank. The child's intense experience was relived emotionally every time Val rejected or betrayed me.

I told myself that this was not Val, whom once I loved and trusted, but now almost feared. It was the multiple sclerosis. It was M.S. talking through her mouth. But words are only words! I didn't believe my own words.

Val did have a point, however. I was not blameless during our forty years together. I was something of a workaholic. Even as I worked in the field of marine electronics, I ran a real estate company for fifteen years, spent many more years studying psychology, and taught myself a little about the craft of writing books.

Directly after our wedding in 1967 our marriage was untarnished by such issues. We lost a baby, Tanya, before she was carried to full term. Two years later Quentin came along and then Melanie. The family was complete.

We moved around a few times in the area north of Wellington, and Val found herself drawn into the mediumistic world.

Val had the ability to communicate with spirit in an amazingly effective way. She provided spiritual healing, sometimes with astonishingly long-term results. She gave readings *(messages from deceased people to their relatives and friends)*. She never charged or accepted donations for all this. On one occasion she told a business acquaintance the names of his children. These and other details, which neither Val nor I possibly could have known, were passed to her by a deceased parent or grandparent. The family belonged to the Indian community in Wellington, and the names of the children were totally foreign to me, and no doubt to her. When next I saw him, he told me that Val had spoken the name of each child, *(which she had never heard)* exactly as his community would say it.

My own abilities were much more modest. One evening while discussing philosophy with my spirit guidance, a young child appeared. She looked about eight but said she was eleven. She had long blonde hair and blue eyes. Her face was solemn, but suddenly lit up into an engaging smile. Tanya had come calling, eleven years after we lost her.

For the next seven months I spent an hour every few days talking to her about her circumstances in spirit. I wrote these into a lecture book. I also ran the information past my guidance occasionally to check its veracity. Sure enough, Miss Eleven acted like a typical eleven-year-old girl. Sometimes she was fanciful, sometimes serious and almost adult, sometimes calculatedly cheeky, and one time moody and negative. This behavior puzzled me, because it ran counter to my preconceived notions. My bewilderment was put to rest by the amused observations of my guidance. Such interactions became understandable as the years went by and my experience increased.

Val and both kids also talked to Tanya at some length, even though Master Nine thought talking to his dead sister was a bit sissy, and Miss Seven had a policy of doing nothing her parents suggested.

The family always resorted to clairaudient *(clear hearing)* psychic communication, where words are perceived as ordinary dictation, but usually illuminated with understanding, at least in my case.

About this time Val became involved with groups to whom she taught mediumistic techniques. She also channeled a teacher, O'Shira, who instructed and counseled group members and visitors from the general community. I found this whole process interesting.

Val slipped into a spontaneous trance and her awareness would be driven by a spirit personality who assumed total control *(trance channeling)*. O'Shira was the principal personality. He was wise, sometimes wickedly witty *(something Val never was)* and discussed information that was far removed from anything Val could have known.

He also had a gift of using allegories, a seemingly unlimited number of them, to highlight the messages he was conveying. They were all new to me.

He also refused to take crap from anyone! On several occasions O'Shira and I disagreed, always respectfully, but in a manner suggesting that philosophically and in every other way we had little in common. Perhaps for that reason Val asked me to leave the group. I wasn't sorry to go. I felt wary and a little uncomfortable with O'Shira and the power he wielded.

He made clear how he was able to control group members as easily as he controlled Val. He also had knowledge about me which nobody else possessed, not even Val.

For example, he told me through the mouth of my entranced wife, small but significant personal details that I never discussed with any other person. There was nothing secretive or sensitive about these details, but the fact he was able to know everything about me was disempowering. I didn't like the feeling that I was a child in his hands.

I suspected I was purposely being pushed out of the group, and that Val and O'Shira had reached an accord along these lines.

At about this time my life took a strange twist, as though in compensation for my divorce from the O'Shira group. I encountered the work of Dr. Francine Shapiro, a senior research fellow at the Mental Health Institute in Palo Alto, California. She had developed a neurological trance technique which was further developed in the United States in such a way that the average person was able to perceive and even communicate with a deceased personality.

Research was taken up by Dr. Allan Botkin, a young psychologist with a background in research who worked in the Chicago Veterans Administration Hospital. This led to the appearance of his 2005 book, *Induced After Death Communication: A New Therapy For Healing Grief and Trauma*.

The book discusses how he trained several dozen professional colleagues in the techniques of Induced After Death Communication (IADC®). They went on to help thousands of their respective clients make contact with dead people.

Their clients came from a broad cross-section of society. They were healthcare professionals including other psychologists, and ex-soldiers suffering from post-traumatic stress disorder. Some had religious beliefs, were skeptics, agnostics or atheists. It worked for people who suffered a recent loss as well as those who recalled an historic loss. IADC® worked with people from a wide variety of racial, cultural and religious backgrounds. People who had brutalized or killed the deceased, or who were victimized by the deceased were able to utilize IADC®. It was established that communication from beyond the grave carried with it an emotional overlay that was healing, forgiving and supportive beyond anything the words or visions conveyed.

Throughout the developmental phase of his new therapy, Dr. Botkin was able to modify and refine his original approach until seventy percent of his clients were able to undergo an IADC® experience.

Consistently and without difficulty, I have replicated Dr. Botkin's findings with clients from my own practice. I carried out extensive empirical research by placing myself in an IADC® trance to powerfully enhance my clairaudient abilities.

I am constantly amazed by the results. IADC® brings with it a new clarity. Not only are the words crisper, whole areas of awareness abruptly emerge and become available. I can receive and understand facts that were beyond my grasp with clairaudience alone. It's as though I am in the room sharing with the communicator, instead of listening from outside the window.

It gave me the means to receive intricate details from my wife as I followed her on her sometimes sad, sometimes enlightening and beautiful journey into another part of the universe.

Back in Val's ward nothing had changed. Still she sat bolt upright. Her eyes remained wide, darting around the room as though begging for help. They seemed especially drawn to the doorway. The doctor reportedly had completed his rounds and decided against intervening. Someone changed the bloodstained towel, but Val continued to hunch over into convulsions and spill more blood from her mouth.

I cornered a nurse. "No," she said, "it would not be possible for you to talk to a doctor." They were short staffed and very busy. "No, it would not be possible to give Val painkillers without the doctor's say-so. It would not be possible to lie her down. The doctor would have to authorize that."

Val's drooping lips flopped from side to side as I tried to move her on the pillows. Her tongue protruded further every time she vomited blood. I placed a hand on her hand. For the last time in her life she glanced in my direction.

I wondered what strength within her soul, within the real Val, prompted her to be in such an awful predicament, the long-term effects of suffering notwithstanding. What did she feel when she noticed the horror on the faces of our young grandchildren, as they watched this huge-eyed stick creature trying vainly to reach out to them, squeezing desperate noises from her mouth? She must have sensed their fear.

Val died alone because I couldn't bear to witness her torment any longer, or live with the rejection she carried as part of her being. Finally I turned my attention to my own survival.

II. The Early Days

Val died in Wellington Hospital at 2 a.m., August 1, 2007.

She came in spirit to see me at home three days later, and gave me a hug.

Two days later I had a vivid dream.

Val and I were at the beach in a family home, which had no existence beyond the dream. I was looking in on my way past. The house was a rotten wreckage due to the ingress of water, partly sunken in the sand and surrounded by debris.

I was aware that I glanced at it in a cursory way before giving Val the go-ahead to buy it. I hadn't even inspected it. I'd taken more notice of the neighboring houses, which were beautiful and situated further back from the beach. Val was left to cope with the wreckage. I knew that the whole mess was my fault.

Two days later I contacted her clairaudiently, but with the process greatly enhanced with IADC®. She admitted she was responsible for the dream. During our marriage, she told me, I had not given her the support necessary because of my work commitments. I was not there much of the time, especially when I was most needed. Therefore, our relationship was a wreck, like the house in my dream. My spirit guidance confirmed Val's involvement.

As I toyed with my cup of cold coffee I thought about Val's words. She was still bent on pushing me away. Talk about letting it all hang out in heaven! Even IADC® had its downside because it made me more sensitive to rejection.

At first glance IADC® seemed so simple. In the normal course of events I merely removed myself from distractions, sat before an open lecture book and started to tap my knees lightly. Within seconds a feeling of calm and relaxation enveloped me as I slipped into a neurological trance. The idea of tapping my knees alternately, left-right, left-right, with about a second in between taps, was to provide neural excitation to those particular nerves within my legs. The nerves throughout the body actually are connected to the brain, so the tapping produces pulsing within the hemispheres of the brain, which in turn initiates a trance state. Memories are typically more intense. Emotions are heightened. Time seems to lose much of its significance and detachment takes hold.

I've done this so often that the process is automatic, like breathing. Even as I begin to tap I open my mind to the clairaudient process, gently reaching for and making myself available to the spirit personality I wish to contact. Nothing happens until I initiate communication with a question or a comment. When the response comes and fills my mind with words I start to write.

I have communicated clairaudiently since I was a young adult, but without the IADC® component. By that time I developed the habit of conversing with various spirits. These included my guidance, individuals who were replaced from time to time as my spiritual education progressed, and my daughter Tanya.

My instruction was furthered in the local Spiritualist Churches in Porirua and Petone which Val and I attended in the early 1980s. Part of this process to expand our understanding involved so-called rescue work, when we made ourselves receptive to spirit personalities who were locked into the proximity of the physical plane by conflict and stress experienced immediately before death. These unhappy individuals, referred to as lost spirits or earthbound spirits, were invited one at a time to take over the body of one of the mediums and talk through his or her mouth. This way the spirit's story could be told and the spirit could then be counseled and guided by the other mediums and encouraged to move in the direction of deceased relatives and friends who awaited their arrival.

On one occasion the spirit was a young mother who was killed in an auto accident, leaving her baby and a preschooler behind. There was no way Samara was going anywhere and leaving her little ones!

The mother's story tumbled from the mouth of a medium while the others talked to her. Tears flowed from Samara-medium, her eyes wide. Her husband had given up work to look after the children, but was not coping. After six months, the entire family still experienced the shock. Her mother wanted to look after the children and this caused a rift between her side of the family and his. Samara watched the drama unfold, and desperately felt the need to intervene, but was unable to make her presence known. She felt redundant and rejected, especially by her own children.

With some difficulty she was persuaded by one of the mediums to reach out for the family members who died. She was to bring them to mind, feel their presence, let go of the children and allow the peace and serenity of spirit to draw her away from the physical. That way she would be able to access the children, but in a more effective way.

After several sessions spanning a fortnight the young mother was agreeable. Abruptly the Samara-medium lost contact. Samara had gone.

Val had become one of those earthbound spirits, locked into the proximity of the physical plane by the stress and conflict of her circumstances during the years at Emmerson House.

Mid-August 2007
Des: Do you mind my communicating and asking questions?
Val: I wouldn't answer if I minded.
Des: Have you met Tanya and O'Shira?
Val: I'm not in a place where they are.
Des: Are you happy?
Val: Not happy or unhappy.
Des: Excited?
Val: No.
Des: Do you think you benefited from your Emmerson experience? Did it happen for a reason?
Val: All experience happens for a reason. I don't know what it is yet.
Des: Is there something you want to say?
Val: I've always loved you, and you have never loved me. I'm not blaming you. You probably did what you could. But that's how I feel.

September 8, 2007
Des: Have things changed during the past three weeks?

Val: Yes, I'm lighter and happier. I'm not in the place where the others are, but I can sense my mother and father. I don't know about Tanya and O'Shira. I'm sort of marking time, not really knowing what is inside my mind. In one way I'm not sure about anything, less sure than when I was in physical. But I am progressing.

Des: May I keep in touch?

Val: If you want to. I don't mind either way.

Des: I feel, perhaps unfairly, that you have always pushed me away. Is it too late for a more loving relationship?

Val: I don't know. As I said, there's a lot I don't know.

September 23, 2007 - Our Fortieth Wedding Anniversary

On this occasion as I sat before my open lecture book, tapping my knees and allowing my mind to drift in the direction of Val's mind, I felt a strange reluctance.

During the past several years on our wedding anniversary, a time when I felt the need to give, my gift was always rebuffed out of hand. I never became accustomed to it. This time was different. Never had I presented a gift to her spirit, or to any spirit. I found myself skirting the subject, pushing away the rejection.

Des: Is there anything I can do to help? Healing or whatever?

Val: Yes there is. You don't try to understand how alone and desperate I feel. That is important, because you are the only link I have. If we can't reach out to each other I have nowhere to go. I'm just as isolated as I was in Emmerson, just me and the walls. Please close your eyes and see me and talk to me. Include me in your life. Nobody has been doing that. It's as though suddenly I have disappeared. The real person inside me feels the same as before.

Des: Do you know what I'm doing right now? Or even thinking?

Val: No Des, I don't. I am here and you are there. There's nobody here with me. It's like Emmerson at night. I am so alone. If you think of me and include me in your life, I'm less alone. No, I'm not miserable or even uncomfortable. I'm just alone. I don't like being alone. I'm not in the place my parents are.

Des: I'm about to put flowers on your grave, as it's our fortieth anniversary, of course. How do you feel about that?

Val: The same as I felt in Emmerson, being told it was our anniversary, that you had brought some flowers for me. Big deal!

Nothing had changed between us! I knew it. But I understood. Although her body was no longer in the high-dependency unit that was Emmerson House, her mind was still there. She lay there, trapped and alone in her predicament. Her most recent memories, especially those that were emotionally charged, became her reality. There she remained. No longer did she have a physical presence, but neither did she have any contact with those in the after-death state.

September 24, 2007

Des: How did you send that dream to me?

Val: I thought my resentful thoughts about you and your mind picked them up in a way you could relate to.

Des: You said you'd like me to reach out to you. The other day I tried. I saw us jogging together while we were at Renown Road, a fantasy of course. Then I visualized us in an imaginary setting like Rivendell in The Lord of the Rings. I'm not sure what you want. I also thought of remembering some times when the kids were young.

Val: Okay Des, you did it all wrong. I just wanted you and me together. Yes, holding hands if you like. I want you to tell me things and then I'll tell you things. I want conversation, nothing more.

Des: Okay I'm with you. *(Despite myself, I found my mind returning to the flowers I brought on the previous day, seeking to change how I felt.)* Were you with me when I put the flowers on your grave?

Val: Yes I was. I saw you return home for water. The orchids look lovely. I have not returned to have a look at them. They will always remain in my mind, and I can see them there.

Des: You mean you can remember them.

Val: No, they are actually there. It's got to do with time. I can just be back when I saw them, and there they are.

Des: I thought of talking to Bernadette and Dawn *(members of Val's group, and close friends)* about the fact you would like people to link with you. How do you feel about that?

Val: I don't want that. I don't want them to feel obligated, and I don't want them to feel guilty or uncomfortable. Just leave this between you and me.

Des: And the family?

Val: Between you and me.

I then used a familiar nickname for her. She became angry, told me she always hated it, and broke off the conversation. I sighed and stared out the window.

My communication with spirit was always a bit of a roller coaster. From time to time they told me things that caused conflict, and sometimes I was criticized. Val was told she would contract a terrible disease, and we were both told we would be involved in an important project involving spirit.

It was proven to me that spirit could block my mind as easily as it could instruct me. I can't remember whether it concerned me then, but it still makes me uncomfortable.

In the end I developed a habit of emotionally walking backwards, away from spirit when I encountered too much conflict, as I have always walked backwards away from Val in order to survive rejection. This prevented me from being a whole, emotional person.

September 27, 2007   1:45 p.m.

Val did not respond to my efforts to communicate on two occasions, which led me to question the viability of the conduit. What if there was something wrong? What if Val had changed her mind? I tried several hours later, and then an hour after that.

Des: Sometimes you do not respond when I try to communicate.
Val: Sometimes I don't feel like responding. Sometimes I feel better than other times.
Des: Are you still aware of the crippled, tetraplegic state you experienced for three years?
Val: That was in my mind as well as my body. It's still in my mind. My surroundings are the same. In Emmerson at

night, I couldn't make known my fear and pain. I couldn't speak, even when a nurse looked into the room. I was so alone and vulnerable. It's still the same.

September 27, 2007   9:05 p.m.
Des: I'm never quite sure when and if you are aware that I am thinking of you.
Val: I'm aware when I want to be aware, and when you want me to be aware, like now.
Des: Would you like me to try to make contact with your parents? Presumably that would help you get out of that awful place.
Val: I'd like that more than anything else.

I wondered why she didn't ask. The answer I received from my guidance was, "Even with IADC®, regardless of your relationship problems with her, you would not have been receptive simply because natural law does not provide for it under those circumstances. But when it was you who initiated the suggestion the circumstances changed. You became receptive." It probably makes sense that those in physical are not expected to guide and support those in spirit. The opposite is the general rule.

September 27, 2007   9:51 p.m.
Des: As you move on I'd really like to keep in touch, and include the details in a book I'm to write. May I include you and talk about your changed circumstances and what you are doing?
Val: Yes, if people stand to benefit.

Val and I had, with our respective guidance, once discussed a project, in which we personally would be involved that was intended to make a change or contribution to our physical community. No details were given. Now that it was happening Val seemed to have no awareness that this was the project. I assumed her present earthbound state of mind, being locked into the Emmerson timeframe, excluded everything that was absent from her mind during that era. Doubtless her horizons would expand again once she moved into spirit proper.

September 28, 2007

I used exaggerated footfalls to initiate the IADC® process as I walked, and asked Val if she knew precisely what I was doing and thinking.

Val: Yes, I know what's in your mind. I know you're out walking. Your mind is on your walk. What you want me to pick up, I pick up.
Des: I'm going to talk to your parents to see if they can help.
Val: Okay.
Des: Later in the day, perhaps. Which reminds me, what awareness of time do you have?
Val: There's no time here. But when I talk to you, you are never far removed from an awareness of time. I pick it up from your mind. I connect to your time.

I talked to Val's mother Aileen, to whom I've talked on occasion during the thirty-five years since she died, using the clairaudience-IADC® interface. She encouraged me to help Val move in their direction, into a lighter and happier place. She said it would happen anyway. Aileen was not too concerned about her daughter's plight, but about what Val had gone through in Emmerson House and before.

I discussed the Aileen dialogue with Val, although she had picked it up from my mind. I asked her to visualize her mother, and be aware of gravitating in their direction. When I asked a short time later how it was going, she said she could do only one thing at a time! I left her to get on with it.

September 29, 2007

Des: Do you live in a place or a no-place?
Val: I live in a no-place.
Des: Could you give me some detail, perhaps?
Val: I seem to be adrift within my emotions, but only the emotions that dominated my years in Emmerson. My memory seems locked in that place. It's as though nothing existed in my life except that swamp of misery and fear.
Des: But you did have visitors in Emmerson.
Val: They were like little islands in the swamp. I could see them and hear them, but that's not where I was. And I was sinking deeper and deeper. Nobody could reach me. I couldn't even scream.
Des: What happened after I suggested you move toward your parents?
Val: I do feel better. I still live in the swamp, but somehow it no longer feels as bad.
Des: Can you sense or communicate with your parents?
Val: No.
Des: I feel that my involvement has more to do with me than with you.
Val: This has always been the case.

Des: Is there any way I can make more of a contribution to your needs?
Val: Your being here is enough.
Des: Did our sometimes unhappy relationship have a meaning? Perhaps serving us both?
Val: I don't know.

October 1, 2007
Des: Were you at your funeral service? What did you think of it?
Val: I saw and felt everything. It was strange, so many people thinking about me. That's what I picked up. Not just the sight, the picture of what happened, although I saw everything, but through the eyes of the people who were there.
Des: Were you sad or disappointed or frightened? Or just exhausted and wrecked when you realized you had passed over?
Val: I was in no shape to do anything more than just drift. I felt sick and hopeless and plain awful. I didn't care.
Des: Have you moved closer to your parents? Could they be more helpful?
Val: Yes, I have sensed Mum and Dad. I do know I won't be in this place forever. That helps. But I'm still angry and hurt and resentful towards you. Sometimes I almost hate you.

October 2, 2007
There were times when I felt like tossing the whole conduit thing away. Bailing out! I studied the new leaves on the silver birch tree outside the window. Why was I doing this to myself? I accepted Val's judgment up to a point. I tended

to blame myself. I always acknowledged the light that shined on me, like the three-year-old on the river bank with his mother.

Beginning the IADC® movements, I made myself psychically receptive, but said nothing.

Val: I'm feeling better now, lighter. I can make out my parents, but that's not the same as being there.

Words formed in my mind that had nothing to do with the conversation. I had emotionally backed into a corner.

Des: It's strange that you should be in a place without day and night, without time, without meals and so on.
Val: I'm in a place dominated by emotions. Meals are not emotions. Time is not an emotion. Night is not an emotion.
Des: You still have thoughts.
Val: Well thoughts cause emotions and emotions cause thoughts. Perhaps they're almost one and the same. Of course I can still think.

Over several days I asked a number of questions. By the time I got around to jotting them down, I forgot most of the discussion.

October 8, 2007
Des: You said that you picked up from my mind only the things I wanted you to pick up. How do you know what I'd want?
Val: Okay, it's as though our minds can be joined. They can also be separate. When they are joined, when we talk, and less so when you just think about me, I know your

opinions and preferences and mindset. So I am guided by those things. I know what you are sending out, and also what has nothing to do with me.

Des: I suspect you put yourself through hell for the last few years for a reason. I probably wouldn't have the strength to do the same. Why did you do this?

Val: I have no answer just at the moment. I am, and I'm here, and I'm starting to understand more. Yes, I've already said I'll keep you informed as I progress.

Des: Can I send you some spiritual healing?

Val: Yes, why not. We'll both learn from the experience.

I directed healing energy to her, although I couldn't remember whether I'd done so for a spirit personality before.

Val: I felt the energy. At that point I became aware that a process is underway that is perfect, that I am being guided, protected and looked after. Everything is okay.

October 9, 2007

Today I talked briefly to Val, mainly just made myself available. She said she continues to feel lighter and freer and more contented.

October 10, 2007

Although I was a bit weary after a long day with clients, I caught up with Val. I was relieved that she sounded much happier, stronger and more confident. She said she had caught up with both her parents.

Val: They were happy to see me, in fact happier than I was to see them. But this was because I'm still burdened, weighed down, oppressed by my physical exertions compared with them. Having said that, my head is clearer, and I feel better and more aware than before.

October 15, 2007

Des: Were your parents together when you met them?

Val: Yes, they were together.

Des: Did you actually see them?

Val: Yes, but I picked up the whole person. Their past physical appearance was just a small part of that. However there was a surprise. They love each other again. The old anger and resentment is gone, the part causing all the problems. The spiritual part of Mum and Dad has always been close. From what I can gather, we create and steer the problems we most need in the physical, because these problems help us to grow in a way we need to grow, or want to grow.

Des: What did they first say to you?

Val: I felt love and acceptance. Then I felt their excitement that at last I had joined them. I felt relief on their part that my suffering was over.

Des: How do you feel about me now, compared with when you first died?

Val: I feel quite different, Des. I have started to shed the part of me that was unfair to you. But I have some way to go. I will change further. I am changing in all sorts of different ways. I am aware of being very excited, although I have been told that there are challenges ahead and always will be. Growth needs to contain some conflict. That can be uncomfortable, especially initially, but will never be a fraction as dreadful as that encountered in physical. One other thing, I said I will always be available to help with your writing. This

might not be possible, for quite complicated and bizarre reasons. I'll do what I can. As in the past there will always be others available to help when needed.
Des: Okay, thank you.

For only the second time in a lot of years we had a hug, the cold knot of unease within me notwithstanding.

III. Moving Away

October 18, 2007
Des: Have you met my spiritual guidance? If so, what do you make of them?
Val: No Des, I have not met them and probably never will. They belong to a different universe. There is a sort of fragmentation that separates groups in spirit. It's a part of the individualizing process that makes every human being different from every other. There is an intimate togetherness existing within every group, which serves the same purpose.

This dialogue became somewhat protracted as I sought to understand more clearly how fragmentation on the one hand and an intimate togetherness on the other hand could come together to help drive individualization. It appears that every so-called group is the equivalent of an incredibly loving and close family, but made up of many hundred members. Emotional affinity is what holds the group together. Communication comprises a mental-emotional linking which involves two or more people. Personal individuality is maintained as in physical life, every person a separate and unique human being.

I asked how this intimate togetherness, which is confined within the group and not shared beyond it, contributes to the individualizing process which Val mentioned.

Every group nurtures and hones its own individuality because the process is exclusive. Each group exists in isolation, influenced by nothing beyond itself. It unfolds creatively. Every group is its own living and evolving oil painting. The individuals within the group are constantly shaped and reshaped by their group identity, spiritually, emotionally and cognitively, even as they build on their uniqueness at the individual level. Every group and individual becomes increasingly different from every other. Individualization!

Consciousness becomes fragmented due to the awareness of every group and the individuality of the people comprising the group, growing more unlike the awareness of every other group.

As this dialogue unfolded and then resolved, I was reminded that Val was given any information that was required, but which she did not possess personally, to pass on to me. Natural law enabled this phenomenon. We discussed it from time to time. I would be given more details in due course.

Later in the day a quite different conversation with Val developed, when I asked whether the widely-acknowledged near-death experience was a valid phenomenon.

Val: This seems to be complicated. The Near Death Experience (NDE) meets a need that exists at a certain time in a certain population. God, by whatever name, creates out of consciousness what is necessary for orderly growth to take place. That's how it works, which doesn't make it right or wrong. It's helpful to understand that when different populations have different needs, they can all be met. Different realities can exist together saying different things. NDEs are a real and valid phenomenon, as are other realities that seem to say almost the opposite.

Des: Exactly how would you define the God you mentioned?

Val: As I see it God is a force, sort of what has caused and what is. God is the stuff, consciousness, which is molded by different minds at different levels and for different purposes. It seems that God is the directing intelligence, creating and indirectly controlling the sea of influence that is consciousness.

October 23, 2007

A problem with the neurotherapeutic technique was becoming apparent. Because my entranced mind tended to flick from one subject to another, the question and answer sequence with Val tended to move about in a disorganized manner.

For example, our discussion about the nature of God was followed immediately by one about the nature of Val's death experience. I have focused primarily on the integrity of the details obtained, as opposed to the dynamics of segueing.

Des: From what I can gather, dying clearly is more than just switching off.

Val: The death experience extends from the time the physical vehicle wears out, at least in my case, to the time in spirit when every emotion and thought has been extracted from the years spent in physical that one chooses to extract.

Des: So you're still dying, even now?

Val: Yes I am.

Des: A strange definition of dying. But I guess you should know.

Val: A word means nothing. I have started to relive the events of my physical life. It's a bit like having a profoundly vivid dream, being in two places or realities at one time, but in this case being able to switch your awareness from one to the other. I feel a compulsion to relive parts of my physical journey, a creative need, an excitement, a fulfillment. It is a part of consciousness, a part of natural law as a person emerges from the shadow of the physical. I embrace experiences that have become increasingly precious to me. Only when this process has been completed has the death experience run its course. Only then have I finished dying.

Des: No doubt it's the same for your mum and dad. What have they said about the death experience, or their lives or anything else? Exactly how do they converse with you?

Val: We talk by merging our minds. What they know and feel, their very personalities, comes into my mind. They pick up the same from my mind. Yes, we talk whenever we want to, much like communicating in the physical. But here it's much more loving and respectful. We discussed the life experiences before they died. I now know what they went through, and their stresses and conflicts. But I also know that this is as much a part of any physical journey, as it was part of Mum and Dad. I am coming to an acceptance of how much they both loved me, and how much of themselves they spent on me. Yes, Dad as well. They did pretty much what they entered physical to do, and that was to merge with negative energy as well as positive, and to build on their energy and on their unique personalities in the process. They put themselves in a particular place at a particular time, and then went about the business of surviving. Each of them developed a whole spectrum of strengths and qualities and resources that were not there before.

October 25, 2007

As I put home-grown orchids on Val's grave I became aware that she was present. I also knew she impressed my mind with the same type of mental-emotional process she and her parents used in order to communicate with one another. The message itself was clear enough. When I thought of her, I needed to seek out happy and harmonious times and step around times of conflict and ill health. I allowed myself to remember times when the children were young before multiple sclerosis set in. A strange serenity, almost elation, rose within me. I knew what to do in the future.

October 29, 2007

Des: I knew you drove the message I got at your grave.
Val: Of course I did. Now you have given the matter some thought, you can see that we both stand to benefit. Your awareness was also steered by your own guidance.

We discussed these issues briefly, and the fact that sooner or later I would encounter my limitations when it came to picking up particularly complex details from Val, even with guidance. The conversation then switched to the people she had recently encountered.

Val: I have met Tanya, other family members, O'Shira, your parents of course, and by extension, their parents. Many others you have never met in physical.
Des: What is my friend O'Shira like?
Val: He is a Being of Light, and as such has responsibilities that ordinary people don't share. These Beings are an incredibly important part of the total Organism, the total human environment. But there's a lot I can't convey at this time.
Des: You can, later on?
Val: It will unfold.
Des: How are you different from him?
Val: As you know, each individual is ordinary while locked into the general proximity of heavy physical matter. But as they move away they become free to unfold their true selves and express who and what they are in spiritual terms.
Des: Then?
Val: Then there is a whole dimension of individual growth that you're barely aware of, relating to so-called evolvement. You don't possess the concepts that would enable us to discuss it in any detail. But we'll proceed as far as we can.

I was quite unable to understand Val's responses, despite the fact that my guidance cut in from time to time to assist. I was aware of silence accompanied by a strange sensation of unease. Before long I knew very well what discomfort my interface with spirit could cause.

IV. Tanya

October 31, 2007   3:30 p.m.

Des: Val, as you know I talked to Tanya on a regular basis for about seven months in 1981. But can you tell me what she's like now?

Val: She is lovely, a lovely little thing. More gentle, more loving, more available than either Quentin or Mel, but strange. I'm still getting my head around her. She shows a lot of light, not surprising after thirty-eight years, but she contains darkness. You are the same. Both the light and the darkness come from physical experiences in one life or another. In physical, the two of you always have been very close, but like magnets, attracting and repelling each other. You both contain something that is tormented, powerful, scary but significant I am told.

Des: So why do you love her?

Val: She is part of my inner group, and furthermore she is mine. I offer no affinity to her darkness, so I do not encounter it. It does not register. I experience only her light.

October 31, 2007 11:00 p.m. Darkness of the Soul
Des: You yourself don't contain darkness?
Val: No. Darkness is not necessarily a bad thing. It means a person has ventured into dark domains, tormented places, and has wrestled with the forces living there. It makes for a more complete human being, but one carrying something of the darkness encountered.
Des: Does that matter, if the person has learned the lesson offered and has risen above it?

Even as the words formed in my mind I was aware that Val would pick up my defensiveness, my sensitivities. I had always felt exposed when talking to spirit. I no longer owned any private thoughts and feelings. It's as though I were hanging naked out the window next to the street. I was still not safe with Val.

Val: The very point I make. The experience will have stamped itself on the individual at every level, for all time, and so has become a part of that soul. Never again will the person be innocent. Even as he has gained something, he has lost something.
Des: I guess that's what individuality is all about.
Val: Quite.
Des: But surely everyone in physical has been sucked into negative energy, that's what the physical is about.
Val: We are talking about degrees of negative activity here, as well as one's personal involvement and cycles that may or may not have become established. There is more involved even than that. A soul with the resources to plunge with premeditation into an intensely negative environment so he is carried away by its savage currents

bears a responsibility that others do not carry. He has been there, lived it and felt it. He knows it. He is able to contribute to the human family in a way that others cannot. For this privilege he will pay a heavy price, because for many lifetimes he will fight his way from the swirling waters, and he will always be marked by darkness.

Des: How does that make me different from one of history's villains, even an Adolf Hitler or his ilk?

Val: You are no different, simply because none of us are different. Every soul immerses itself in that awful flow. Whether in the shallows or among the fierce undertows and deadly current that rends the middle of the torrent, depends on the strength or will of the soul. More to the point, Des, look at what you are now. You hold to yourself an adage that you respect and follow in your daily life, *be the world you want to see*. That defines you. I think that's good enough.

December 4, 2007 Intelligence in Spirit

Des: How were you given help to answer that question, and others? What process is involved? Not only do you know more than was the case in physical, but your opinions have changed.

Val: As you've discussed with your guidance, I make myself available and receptive, pretty much as you are doing right now. The answers are then presented to me. Natural law provides the answers, as long as there is justification for this. The process is one where a need is met if there is sufficient reason for the need to be met.

Des: When you say natural law, you mean the people who drive the conduit.

Val: Yes. Natural law is expressing itself through them. The stepping process also comes into it, where evolved beings step information and perspectives to lower levels of consciousness to make details available to those in spirit with a direct link to the physical. What I experience is a situation where your questions are answered with details filling my mind. Sometimes the details are different from my own understanding.

Des: At which point does the new information become yours at the personal level?

Val: Whole areas of knowledge fall into place. Your role within the conduit provides you with the entitlement to ask these questions. I then have the entitlement to possess the answers. In the normal course of events, the stepping system contains a mechanism in which, at every step the personality involved interprets the flow of intelligence while passing it down the line. The intelligence loses integrity, becoming less and less like the original. This is so with the endless stream of intelligence which always has moved into the physical, much of which does not originate from the Beings with responsibility for the Organism.

Des: It comes from further down the line? There must be a reason for that imperfection.

Val: Certainly. The version of the intelligence made available at the physical level is one to which those in physical are able to relate, make sense of, and put to use. A spirit in close proximity to heavy matter has a perspective only slightly removed from that of the physical plane.

Des: And the situation with the conduit?

Val: The conduit was put in place by those representing the Organism itself, and serves its aspirations. The people providing its intelligence decide what those in physical need, what they can relate to, and how it will be presented. They have the enablement. There is a much more direct link between the source and me, and between the source and you.

December 19, 2007 Embryos That Are Lost

Des: It seems likely that many couples lose a dozen or more embryos over the years, and know nothing about it. Presumably each results in a personality in spirit. We might have numerous Tanyas in spirit, all of them her siblings.

Val: This is not the case. Much more is involved than merely a physical act that creates a baby. Take Tanya. She was part of our mind. We were aware of having lost her. Later we all communicated with her, got to know Miss Eleven, and included her in our family. Even with a typical family, providing at least one parent is aware of the unborn baby *(invariably the mother)*, that awareness creates a link with a particular spirit personality. Whether or not the baby is destined to die, the spirit progressively moves into physical. In the event that the baby passes over, it is accepted into the family environment in spirit. Had I not been aware of losing Tanya, nothing would have existed at the mental/emotional level to attract a spirit. There would be no Tanya.

Des: Did the Tanya spirit already belong to the family, the inner part of the group?

Val: Oh yes. But she was far removed from heavy matter. She processed everything associated with her previous incarnation and became distant from such concerns.

Des: Even though there's no such thing as time in the physical sense?
Val: That's right. It's important to remember that she was and is her own creation, while also being a creation of our minds. You cannot create without an awareness of creating. We created her, and she facilitated that.
Des: Exactly what did we create?
Val: A mental/emotional mold or matrix *(within a matrix, within a matrix, within a matrix)* that was able to shape, within very strict boundaries, the spirit presenting itself to us.
Des: I can't quite get my head around it.
Val: We created, at one level or another, in order to progress Tanya's agenda and to a lesser extent, our own. We were always creating Tanya's and our own personal individualization and unfoldment. Tanya chose a developmental journey in spirit rather than in physical, because it suited her purpose. We helped make this possible.
Des: And you suggest that her premature departure into spirit served our purpose as well?
Val: You and I are discussing her right now. We're learning, not by chance. She is furthering our work with the conduit.
Des: But not every family is tied into the conduit.
Val: Every family is unique. Every journey is unique. The same principles apply.
Des: Is she familiar with the stuff we're talking about?
Val: Up to a point, but she is still processing her physical experience.
Des: Nothing is simple, is it?
Val: Hah! That's only the three-times table, Des.

December 28, 2007 Conflicts in Spirit

Des: Do you encounter differences of opinion or conflicts in your environment, Val?

Val: The answer is yes and no. Where there is personal growth there will be conflict. That's where growth comes from, the way in which we identify and reconcile and resolve the conflict. What you refer to in physical as conflict, we don't encounter. We are drawn together by positive bonds. I can flow into the mind of the person I am with and vice versa. We understand the other's deepest viewpoint. We empathize, feel kinship and an affinity. But we are all in the process of becoming less and less like any other human being who has ever lived.

Des: That sounds like a contradiction.

Val: It doesn't have to be. Think about it.

Des: Can you give me an example? Maybe a difference of opinion between you and Tanya?

Val: We did have a difference, which could hardly be called even a tiny conflict. It was about you. It went like this. My life experiences with you have been complex and sometimes difficult for many reasons. My present activities with the conduit, and yours, were shaped in some measure by our past relationship. I understand this completely now.

But from Tanya's viewpoint you are exciting and a bit mysterious. Of course she lacks any understanding of our relationship issues and what they offered us. Tanya fails to acknowledge that her only understanding of life in the physical comes from a process we will discuss shortly, but that's not really life in the physical. If she cannot understand her parents' dilemmas, she sees you in a romantic light. She takes your side. I don't mind, even though I'm still in the shadow of physical experience. More to the point, this difference is what you asked about.

Des: Thank you. You were saying that Tanya understands life through a process that... I've got some idea of what's involved, but nothing more.

Val: From the time she was a young child in spirit she's been learning about the physical. She was taught mainly by two families, yours and mine. She talked, listened, enjoyed, and was enjoyed as she continued to learn. In that way she grew a personality and an understanding of herself and the physical, but always within the matrix that you and I had woven around her. She was ours. As her mind fused with a family member with whom she was communicating, she was able to inject herself on occasion and by prearrangement, into the other's lifetime in physical. Over time she embraced a whole spectrum of experiences with different people. In piggy-back terms she has lived not one, but many physical journeys. In the absence of any direct physical life of her own, she was defined and shaped by the physical lives of others. It is important to understand that she was immersed emotionally and in other ways. However, because the group members involved loved and protected her as a natural reaction, they provided an incomplete picture of life in the physical.

Although this selective lack of detail became much less as her experience expanded, she lacks completely what would be called in physical, street smarts. She is like a very wise, innocent child. You can see how my life, sometimes brutal during the final few years, departed from anything she could understand. It is the same as with our relationship. The end result is no reduction in love between Tanya and me, the sort of unconditional closeness that is never encountered in physical, but with a tiny hint of conflict.

Des: No doubt this process helps bring group members closer together.

Val: That's right, Des. Of course communication is restricted to group members because nothing else registers. As the process reinforces group affinity, especially within the inner group, it also develops an increasingly powerful group identity that plays into the hands of the law of individualization, simply because every group is doing the same.

November 2, 2007 The Human Organism

Des: Every group added together is the Human Organism. Can you tell me something about that?

Val: The Organism includes spirit and physical. This term speaks to a significant reality. Humanity is a single body. But it is much more. It is a sea of awareness, but only a tiny part of consciousness. It is a thought and a memory. It is an emotional and analytical reservoir, a link with what is contained within it and what exists beyond it. It is also very much more than can be expressed through this conduit.

Des: This feels a bit like philosophizing on the hole in a donut.

Val: As this book progresses your questions will be answered more fully.

Des: Their questions. I'm prompted, almost as though I have a cue card.

Val: That's right, although they never interfere with your free will.

Des: Who does the prompting? Does it come from the top of the evolutionary ladder?

Val: That depends on the particular information. They are all just people.

Des: To whom does Mr. Big answer?

Val: We're all part of a single body, the Organism. Some people have developed resources that enable them to take more responsibility.

Des: How are the Beings of Light we've discussed different from more modest individuals?

Val: As a parent is different from a child.

November 10, 2007 Ghosts

Des: Sometimes it might be easier to understand the world by kicking at the dirt, instead of philosophizing on the stars. When we talked about your funeral, you said that you could link into the scene, see the physical world, through the senses of the people who were there. Presumably it's the same with everyone in spirit. This concept doesn't explain how so-called ghosts are almost part of the physical environment. They can be observed by individuals with no connection to the ghost.

Val: Spirit personalities always have a link with family in the physical. In one sense the spirit and the physical family members are part of the same body, although individuality remains completely intact. Being one with you, I was able to use your eyes at my funeral to see what was going on. I could experience the event through the emotions and thoughts of almost everyone present.

Des: But those people present weren't all family members.

Val: Most were, actually. Those not belonging to the genetic family, with the odd exception, had formed a bond with me that always will make them one with me. Family is far more than a bloodline. It is love, affinity and shared experiences. To that extent, at least some of those present were family because of these bonds. The link with my close friends, many of whom were in my psychic groups, drew them into the inner circle in spirit to which I belong.

But you asked about ghosts. The dead person is still tied completely into the physical world. The vibrations are so coarse that a sensitive person, even a tourist visiting a haunted house can almost see the ghost. A completely earthbound spirit, locked into even more profoundly negative emotions, sees nothing of the physical environment, and is still living within memory. Even if the house in which the spirit lived burned down and a modern house concepted in its place, the spirit continues to dwell within the house that no longer exists because it continues to exist in the mind. There is no such thing as time. Spirit is back there. Physical people living within the modern house may glimpse the wandering spirit pass through walls. The spirit has no awareness of the modern house or its inhabitants, which do not exist for spirit.

Des: Then what about evil or angry spirits who are said to attack people, cause objects to move or whatever?

Val: Depending on the intensity of the negative emotions present at the time of death, a different natural law may enable the person's spirit to break through into the present, be aware of and interact with the occupants of the modern house. This could be so if the spirit personality is consumed with rage or vindictiveness. The greater the negative emotions, the coarser the individual's vibrations, and the greater the affinity with the physical. Expression at the physical level, therefore, is possible. Coarse vibrations enable contact to be made between the spirit and people in the physical. It could be added that this phenomenon is rarely experienced. Exaggeration in the telling is a significant factor.

Des: Natural law seems to be an almost contrived, certainly convenient, device to explain pretty much anything and everything.

Val: You do have a point, Des. The term natural law is an effort to make an intricate web of influences within the fabric of consciousness understandable. Use the word God if you like. A word means nothing in itself. Even in the highest reaches of spirit it is possible to identify the barely knowable only by falling back on analogies. The term natural law is nothing more than an analogy.

January 10, 2008 Failed Spiritual Healing?

Des: I saw a program on television a year ago about the Brazilian healer called John of God while he was working in Lower Hutt some months before you died. You actually were there with your friend Bernadette, although I didn't see you. Why didn't John of God heal you?

Val: He did! Although, at the time, my course had been set and nothing could change it, he gave me a level of acceptance, of reconciliation, of peace. The raw terror about my predicament became more manageable. The sense of betrayal started to ebb away. The physical pain abated. I was more free and healed.

January 13, 2008 Male and Female in Spirit
Des: I understand that all spirit personalities contain both male and female energy. Is this correct?
Val: Immediately after death a spirit continues to identify itself with the familiar gender, growing away from that exclusiveness only as he or she moves further from physical matter. But you are thinking now of O'Shira. He identified as a male in the physical because it was convenient to meet certain expectations.

As is usual nowadays, we have a brief hug before going our respective ways.

V. Animals in Spirit

November 12, 2007

Des: Presumably you have caught up with the moggies, Belle, Gremlin, Nick, Twinkle, Boots and Whisky.

Val: Yes I have. But that introduces an interesting subject. When the cats were in the physical, they encountered stress and also caused stress. Whisky was killed by a dog, an incident no doubt causing him some stress. Because I loved him so much I was greatly stressed. When I encountered the animals one at a time, we merged as I thought of them. They were pure; they were not locked into that negative physical energy. I was able to love them completely, because deep down I was not bracing myself, knowing that sooner or later I would lose them. But even in this realm as I move further and further from the influence of the physical, I know that in time I will shed any need for the company of my cats. I will outgrow the need as I become more self-contained and balanced and whole. In a completely different way I will internalize them so they will always be a part of me.

Des: Does the cat not gravitate away from its physical life as people do?

VAL: The mandate of this conduit is to move general information through it. Nothing more is appropriate at this time.

Des: That doesn't sound like Val.

Val: It is now. In personal terms I find myself either distancing myself from the conduit, from you, or drawing closer to it, depending on the nature of the information. In the case of my cats, though, I can say that once removed from negative physical energy nature is beautiful, perfect, and gentle. My cats are in safe hands and always will be.

Des: Have you always moved towards and away from the conduit?

Val: Well, the nature of our talks is changing, and will continue to do so, tending to become more complex and having less to do with Des-Val stuff. The personal me moves either closer or further away, while the channel I provide remains in place.

Des: Who was talking before?

Val: You're going to find out, Des.

December 13, 2007 The Symbol and the Cat

Des: When I did IADC® with our beautiful ginger cat Nicholas after he died, why did he send me a symbol? Just a paw print and nothing more. A cat doesn't know about symbols.

Val: I think your guidance already has given you an answer, Des. You have a particular role in life, as many people do. In your case no opportunity is missed to teach you. The contact with Nick was an opportunity. Clearly the

IADC® message came from more than just Nick. A symbol is significant. On the one hand, so much of your daily life in physical presents itself as one symbol or another. You create symbols with your awareness of the external environment, family, country and ethnicity, democracy, the Church, your physical body, social status, even your car. You embrace these symbols because they satisfy a need within you. They provide roots for you, a framework enabling you to relate to others. It is all part of the physical.

Think about it. Nick taught you quite a lot. Nobody could own Nick. He was not only fun-loving, loyal and intelligent, he was independent. He came and went as he chose, even as the paw print appeared then disappeared despite your wishes for something more. Nick demanded respect. For brief periods he actually dominated your external and internal environments.

Des: How was I to work all that out from a one-second experience with IADC®?

Val: Well, you have. There are no accidents or coincidences. Things happen for a reason according to natural law. Were it not for the IADC® with our beautiful Nicholas, this dialogue would not be taking place. On occasion while playing with him, you both loved and respected your internal and external environments, you were comfortable with them. And Nick was only a cat. Good night, Des.

November 13, 2007 Just What Are Animals?

Val: That's an interesting question. Obviously they share the planet with us, and so they are a part of the greater planetary organism. But a different focus tells another story. In a narrow context animals are the more evolved life form. Animal behavior is driven by instinct. Instinct comes from the collective mind of that particular animal species. It's almost possible to say that there is only one domestic cat in the world and one domestic dog and one giraffe, and so on, and that every species shares a single instinctive mind. It is not possible for an individual animal to act in a way that is against the collective instinct, although unusual environmental pressures will produce unusual adaptive behaviors. Selective breeding can also bend behavior.

People are uniquely different. Although there are patterns of instinctive behavior, steered in some measure by one's society, it is overwhelmed at the individual level by the thinking mind. This splits humans off from the animal kingdom.

Other factors do as well. Animals do not have free will that is removed from instinct. Humans do. Humans are able to initiate bad or wrong *(immature)* behavior and self-destructive behavior in the physical, individually and collectively. Human beings create themselves because of the consequences of their activities. People are responsible for what they do. This is how they create what they are. Not so, animals. It could be said that this has already been done for them.

It could be suggested that every human being is the equivalent of an entire animal species. With animals, though, the process has reached perfection so far as the relationship with their surroundings is concerned. Animals mesh with an environment principally designed to unfold human potential. But with people the process of individualization and evolvement is very much a work in progress. Mistakes continue to be made because learning proceeds according to the process of trial and error. Errors lead to warfare, religious intolerance, mass poverty and starvation; and at the individual level to psychological health and social problems.

In turn this conflict produces suffering, and thereafter empathy which teaches lessons and eventually damps down the negative excesses.

January 23, 2008 Experiencing the Physical

Des: Do you take satisfaction from the contributions you made with your spiritual channeling groups, psychic readings, spiritual healing and counseling? What do you make of the awful experiences you endured during the last few years?

Val: I take enormous satisfaction from every second I spent in physical, whether I was happy or not. I now know that every second was a profound privilege. I created within me what had not existed. Every thought, emotion and activity, no matter how fleeting, gave birth to something that will last forever. It contributes to the family here and to the greater group. Concerning my psychic gifts, we are all given the means to make a positive contribution. I made the most of what I had. You are doing the same. Many do not. As far as my bad experiences in physical go, this is an inescapable part of life on that plane, even if the types of suffering vary.

November 16, 2007 Relationships in Spirit

Des: Apparently you have met my parents. How have they changed? Were they surprised to see you?

Val: Yes they were surprised. I was a little taken back by that. I thought that devoid of time they would know about my circumstances. But they belong to quite another group from me, and the somewhat remote relationship between the two groups meant they did not expect me. The main link between the groups is our family, you and me and the youngsters.

I think the very insular personality of your parents also contributed. I'm not sure how they have changed. I'm still learning. There always has been a distance between them and me. But the connection between groups, and even within a single group, is quite complicated. Within the same group there is an intense attraction, almost a oneness, more so in parts of the group than in others.

In the more remote reaches of the group that affinity falls away, until eventually those people seem to have more in common with other groups.

Des: Is there a hint of competition or lack of empathy?

Val: Oh no. It's more a relative lack of closeness and intimacy and oneness. Affinity becomes greater the further into your own group you move. Central within any group is the immediate family, which produces a positive emotional intensity that is not encountered in the physical.

Des: Why don't you use the word love, Val?

Val: Des! They are your words, not mine! My thoughts are clothed with your words.

Des: You're right, of course.

November 18, 2007

Des: How have your circumstances changed since you first

Val: contacted your parents, O'Shira, Tanya and others?
Val: That's easy to answer. Nothing much has changed. In one way we interact in the type of environment you would recognize. In another way, within that environment, there is a fluid exchange of information, emotions, recollections, questions and answers and all the rest of it. The type of information and the depth of understanding and satisfaction involved are expanding all the time. I still have little idea of what lies ahead. I also have a number of deep and searching questions. The answers will become available one way or another only when I am able to comprehend them in a meaningful way.

November 20, 2008 Des' Communication
Des: Exactly what is the relationship between all this information you have been giving me, and the simplified version of it my guidance provided over the years? There are differences. How do I reconcile these?

For much of our adult lives Val and I linked with our respective spiritual guidance. This phenomenon comprises a unique interface between one or more discarnate personalities and an individual in physical. *(Within the international Spiritualist community there are slightly different views and definitions on this subject.)* The purpose of this psychic interface is to make available to the physical person, perspectives, insights and concrete information, to support the agenda he or she came to physical to pursue. People have different ways in which they can receive the discarnate input. Some individuals are consciously aware of the process and others are not.

Val: There is no comparing to be done. They come from the same source. The two streams of information might seem to differ at first glance. You use IADC® when talking to me, which provides far more detail and clarity than was available with your guidance. As you know, with them your psychic link alone was sufficient to introduce and develop a framework of concepts on which we are now able to build. You still use your guidance to clarify various issues. Different agendas and roles are involved now. Your guidance prepared you to function within the conduit. Now the two of us are part of a movement which uses the conduit.

VI. Defining a Spirit

January 21, 2008

Des: I am interested in the nature of the soul or spirit or higher self. Can you help me?

Val: Within the body of consciousness there exist individualized parts that are members of the human race. That's what we are, you and I.

Des: Units of awareness, free will, embedded in the body of consciousness.

Val: We are actually part of the total, as a drop of water is part of the river. In your case, a part of you is focused in physical, while another part is focused in spirit. In my case, a much larger part is in spirit, but not all of it because I am still processing my physical life.

Des: The physical is just an add-on to spirit?

Val: The physical you is like a rowing boat in the middle of the Pacific Ocean. The spirit you is the Pacific. Both are parts of the total. Each person, whether in physical or spirit, is constantly evolving and individualizing. Past lives are part of a parade of existences in the physical which all take place at the same split second of time. There is no time, as we've discussed.

The term used to describe a spirit is just that, a term. In various explanations to you, the terms spirit, soul, higher self and overself have been used loosely. An analogy within an analogy can be looked at to define each one if necessary.

Consciousness is much more than we have touched on. It is not only endless, but also has infinite potential and therefore is quite unknowable. What we do is put together a few facts that we are able to understand. These make up a model, concept or paradigm, a framework that we are able to relate to and call the universe or consciousness. That is all we have. This is all that humanity knows of itself. We use the framework to answer your questions.

Des: The answers are channeled via a stepping process, of course.

Val: Yes, in the normal course of events, from the upper reaches of the Organism. We'll talk in more detail about the stepping process in due course.

January 24, 2008 Spirit is Humorless?

Des: In communicating with spirit, with the exception of you, the people I have talked to seem so serious and focused, almost humorless, even when my rapier-like wit is wielded. Is there any fun and humor in those hallowed halls?

Val: The answer is simple enough. Love is love. When you are caring for a baby or a child, your time and energies are not wasted on trying to be funny. In one context or another humor can be self-indulgent and immature, or even a defensive or coping strategy. Here that is not necessary. But that doesn't mean we fail to understand humor. There is another consideration, though. Whenever we communicate with you, energy is used. The energy is available only if its use is justified, only if there is a good reason for the communication. There would be little reason if we exchanged jokes.

January 26, 2008 Reflections on a Physical Life

Des: Do you feel any particular link with our past homes? Worcester, Kahu, Awanui, the motels, Renown? Even this place or Emmerson? Waikanae cemetery?

Val: I feel the same type of link that I feel about my physical life in general. The physical always seems oppressive and dark, heavy and brooding, thoroughly unpleasant, while at the same time vastly important. The flashes of love are an exception, appearing like beams of sunlight coming through the branches of a tree and lighting up the darkness of the forest floor.

The houses obviously marked different phases of my life, and so different lessons were offered. Different parts of me were unfolded. There is little difference between one set of walls and another, one lawn and another, one shopping center and another. They were just aspects of my physical life. Sure, they contained different emotions, but the whole physical journey was a play of emotions, like the play of light on the forest floor.

Des: Without light I guess there would be only darkness.

Val: Without love there would be only darkness. Our motels were different, but even they contained interplays of emotion. Emmerson House. That was a very severe time for me, to an extent that I don't think you understood. But essentially it was my choice. You responded with loyalty and commendable principles. Your interface with me during that time was your choice. A final comment though. My time in the physical is not over yet, because I'm still dwelling within its shadows, revisiting my past, exploring further growth experiences.

January 28, 2008 Spirit Continues Involvement with Physical

Des: I have another question. As you mentioned, and as I discussed with my guidance in more detail, a spirit continues to interact with its physical life in a number of ways.
    (a) By reliving some or all of its life events
    (b) By exploring possible futures
    (c) Other interactions.
Can you provide specific details about them all?

Val: Reliving physical events. There is a built-in need to explore the physical life left behind, as there is a built-in need to breathe while living in the physical. Recently my mind has taken me back to revisit all manner of highways and byways, in a way that fascinates me as it never did while I was in physical. I am captivated by the process, partly because I feel an unfamiliar empowerment. I can come and go as I wish. I am not imprisoned. I am aware of what the physical undertaking offers me, so I feel immersed in an incredibly powerful creative act. The opportunity to relive every moment of every event offers areas of knowledge that are unique. The spirit's growth and individualization expand.

As the spirit continues to gravitate further from the harsh influence of heavy matter, different areas of awareness, different lessons, are provided from a reliving of exactly the same events. The person becomes receptive to various perspectives as he continues to shed coarse vibrations and becomes more distanced from negative energy.

Let's consider one month after death, and then one year after death. At the one month point, typically the spirit feels very much as he did before passing over. He might experience anger, resentment, egotism, other negative emotions and the usual spectrum of positive emotions. Overlaying these feelings is a serenity, a relief, and a sense of being safe.

At the one year point things have changed. There is a permeating love and gentleness, a sense of forgiveness. This is reinforced by ongoing communication with other spirit personalities. When revisiting events from the physical lifetime it is from a different emotional standpoint. One is able to pick up lessons, come to conclusions, deliver judgments and generally use a particular event in a different manner. He sucks from each morsel hungrily for this is how he perceives the individual moments of his physical journey that previously eluded him.

When the spirit has moved a certain distance from the physical, he is able to do something quite different. He can gather all the information together and obtain a more complete oversight. He navigates within the entire lifetime and makes relative judgments, balances conclusions, evaluates areas of maturity and immaturity, determines how they came about, then stands back and observes unfolding patterns. Every decision in physical produces its own outcome. Let us focus on major decisions. Each actually produces a unique future for the decision-maker. A different person flows from and is progressively shaped by every major decision because of the influence on him of the new future that his decision has opened.

Every future develops its own unique person and likewise the fellow travelers inhabiting the new future. By definition every future comprises its own universe or reality. It stands to reason that every future is fragmented along its time-line again and again as the branches of a tree continually divide. This happens within every future as further decisions are made. Other futures are created. Within these more decisions are made and more futures given form and a life of their own. The inhabitant of every future is as real as you are now. Of course you are one of them. They all live and die. Every you lives in a single soul, although there is a separate spirit, for every physical life. Every you contributes to infinite webs of consciousness before and after physical death.

In spirit you will explore not merely one Des' lifetime in physical, but every Des' lifetime. In other words you will relive every significant moment of every future, and take from the complete experience what is offered.

Des: But what are all the other Des' doing while I'm scratching around in their lives like an old hen? Will they pick up my presence?

Val: While the individual remains within the influence of the last physical journey, as I am at present and will be for quite a long time, he is restricted to a limited awareness.

Until I finish processing my physical life as I understood it while in the physical, it represents the limits of my awareness. It is the same for every you. A following phase of evolvement involves the awareness of every Des coming together, some having died in childhood.

Des: It is hard to imagine that a child can make major decisions.

Val: A child can willfully run across the road and get run over, or fish where he's not supposed to, and fall in a pond. Or she can end up pregnant or crash her car.

Des: Are these major decisions?

Val: If the child ends up dead, it's fairly major.

Des: When I married you I didn't realize I'd be marrying thousands of people!

Val: Lucky you. But there are thousands of Des' involved. When we married we each occupied a single future. As time went by, individual and shared decisions caused a fragmentation, as we created an increasing number of different futures or realities for each of us. The nature of our relationship changed as the parties sharing the relationship changed.

Des: What of those shared and minor decisions? It's hard to see the same principle holding.

Val: At this point our discussion encounters a problem, several in fact.

(1) You lack a sufficiently comprehensive language of common concepts to understand our responses.

(2) The analogies being used to create these answers are intended only for the broadest concepts.

These we have covered on the subject.

(3) This conduit was put together to serve a particular

agenda. A tiny spectrum of information is to be conveyed to the physical at this time.

Details about minor, shared and childhood decisions do not fall within that spectrum, that agenda. Therefore they are not available.

Concerning other spirit-physical interactions, spirit personalities in the normal course of events communicate at length with one another and share experiences. Many of these relate to their past physical lives. Every individual's physical life has a significant influence on those within the inner group, especially bearing in mind the spontaneous and emotionally complete nature of the communication. An individual will communicate frequently with everyone in the inner group but less often in the wider group. Emotionally and in other ways, every spirit is able to dwell within the physical lifetime of every other. This is one way in which the character and uniqueness of a group is formed.

Des: Okay, thank you.

January 29, 2008 Reincarnation

Des: I guess another area of involvement with physical life is the question of reincarnation. Is there any consensus about reincarnation?

Val: There are as many theories or interpretations as there are people with an interest in the subject. In fact reincarnation is a simplification to explain something that is not simple.

Des: I was afraid of that.

Val: Consciousness is a medium that is all about creating. It relies on the process of creating, and the process of creating relies on it. People create a reality by believing in it. A number of people reinforce that. A large number of people, some in physical and some in spirit, feeding a belief structure give it a reality that cannot be denied. This applies to reincarnation, but not only reincarnation. The question could be asked as to what or who is being returned to the physical plane time and again as part of the incarnating or reincarnating experience. When John Smith dies he will never be returned to the physical! What is returned, perhaps, is a John Smith equipped with very much more wisdom, almost a different life form in some cases, and also stripped of some of his negative parts.

To further confuse the issue, is the fact that bits of John Smith inhabit other individuals returning to physical, even as John has come to internalize or contain the essence of others in his group but especially his family group. *(To understand how this happens refer back to the notes on Other Spirit-Physical Interactions.)* To confuse the confusion one could say that there is no time as you understand it, meaning that every past lifetime is taking place at this split second of time.

Des: I understand that while in physical, you personally never accepted the existence of reincarnation, at least the popular spin on it.

Val: Well, I have learned a lot since then. More to the point though, the information that is being conveyed to you has little to do with me. I am passing on what I receive.

Des: But you must have a level of acceptance of the points made.

Val: Only when they have been made do they become mine.

Des: I can see that, thank you. How come an individual is so positive and loving in spirit, but sometimes becomes bad again when he decides to gain more evolvement by reincarnating? Surely he's more or less the same person, notwithstanding what you've just told me.

Val: Let's look at the physical environment he enters. It is like a coin with two sides, or an emotional division with two different faces. That is, it is made up of interplay of negative and positive energies producing negative and positive emotions, and the resulting behavior. Something strange happens when the person returns to physical and fuses with negative energy. It awakens within him something of the same negative tendencies and appetites he carried when last in physical form, when last in the proximity of negative energy, just as the positive energy of spirit unfolded within him the loving and benign attitudes that are a deep and basic part of every human being.

Des: Presumably a Being of Light living in the physical world has the resources to rise above the worst of the negative energy, while more ordinary individuals can even be destroyed by it.

Val: Destroyed is not the right word. A person benefits enormously from a physical journey, whatever direction it takes. But an evolved personality does not need the harshest of the learning experiences so necessary for most other individuals. Therefore he does not attract them to himself. But there are exceptions. If he is swept away by catastrophe or personal tragedy, he has chosen these harsh experiences in service to the Organism and not his personal unfoldment.

January 29, 2008 More about the Vexing Question of Time

Des: Okay, there is no time so far as reincarnation is concerned. But in spirit, clearly there are trains of cause and effect. You might do or say something and consequences flow from that activity. How can this be so if there is no time?

Val: Time is one of the subjects that is pretty much impossible for us to discuss, because you lack the concepts involving no time. I could not help you to relate to a color you had never seen.

Des: I suppose if it were intended that we talk about time, the necessary concepts or words would have been developed over the years as part of the conduit.

Val: Precisely. The conduit has been shaped and refined painstakingly, as you are well aware. For a definition of time to be available, a complex analogy would be necessary. The subject of time simply does not justify such expenditure. It is not an important part of the agenda.

Des: Perhaps some aspects of time can be discussed? Something I've been thinking about. Theory has it that following the so-called "big bang" the physical universe has continued to expand. I was told by my guidance that consciousness likewise is an expanding phenomenon. Is there any relationship between the two?

Val: No. Consciousness, the ultimate law or matrix of natural law, is growing and changing as those contributing to it and comprising consciousness grow and change.

Des: You mean the human race?

Val: Humanity is only a tiny part of the process. Consciousness is an energy made up of every life form.
Des: Including rocks, insects, and trees?
Val: Certainly. And the planet as a whole, the sun itself, other galaxies, and also life forms existing in other dimensions. With every thought and every experience consciousness expands, faster and faster. It always has and always will.

January 30, 2008 Lucky Charms

Des: I'm reluctant to ask this question, but I have been bid to do so. Do lucky charms work? If so, how and why?
Val: Yes, they often do Des, your slight dismay at the answer regardless. Directly and indirectly, by one means or another, for one reason or another, people create a need within themselves. That need may be for security, a sense of being safe. Other needs may involve success, or the avoidance of failure, comfort or a sense of structure. When these needs are met people generally feel better.

    To meet these emotional needs, people resort to all sorts of behavior. Some become very controlling or manipulative, submissive, even resort to escapist behavior. Other people resort to carrying a lucky charm to which they attribute a symbolic quality. They are creating within their minds something that will meet their needs. However at a different level they are deferring to a law of nature which says, if the need is sufficiently compelling, the creative agency that is consciousness will meet it. A part of consciousness creates a need. Another part meets it.

November 21, 2007 Christmas in Spirit

Des: What does Christmas in the physical mean to you, and what does Christmas in spirit mean to you?

Val: If Christmas coincides with people being uplifted and supported and given satisfaction in the physical, it is a very pleasing event. If Christmas is a lonely or sad time, we feel for the person if we have a group connection. The strength of our feelings is linked to the strength of the connection. If there is no personal connection we feel nothing. There is nothing to register. But in spiritual and philosophical terms we are empathetic. Regarding the religious significance, because religion has been invented to meet valid needs, collective and individual, as part of the inevitable growing process, it is no less real. Everything has been created because everything is part of consciousness, and consciousness is creating and being created. In spirit we accept what is, and the infinite natural laws within consciousness creating it.

December 23, 2007 2:30 p.m. More about Christmas

Des: With Christmas almost on us, I've been wondering what you will be doing on Christmas Day. Anything different? Why?

Val: No Des, I'll be doing nothing out of the ordinary. I love doing just what I'm doing. But there is a difference when Christmas Day comes along. A radiant energy can be felt emanating from the physical. This is not surprising, as the two realms are just part of the same country so we are aware of that energy. Christmas Day is different and feels different. Those in physical in predominantly Christian countries, or at least a great

many of them, produce an emotional uplift because they subscribe to that particular belief system.
Des: You wouldn't experience very much of that uplifting, I guess, because you receive energy from only the tiny number of people in physical who belong to your group.
Val: That is not correct. Directly and indirectly, members of the greater group have connections to people in physical from a vast assortment of groups throughout the world. Collectively they pick up the energy which then becomes available to all members of our greater group.
Des: I see.
Val: Many people in physical see Christmas merely as family time, an opportunity to enjoy the company of a larger than usual number of family members. But that is okay. Love is love, even if the focus shifts at Christmas. People have always created symbols in order to relate positively or negatively. Christmas is one such symbol. On Christmas Day people create an energy infrastructure that did not exist a few days before. They create something within themselves individually and collectively. They create! Everything is a creation within a creation within a creation, forever.

December 23, 2007 9:15 p.m. Negative Creations
Des: Can you think of any negative creations?
Val: That won't be hard. A modern-day holy war is a negative creation, in which both sides sincerely believe in their cause, and some people are willing to die or kill for it. Materialism, elitism, the unfeeling exercise of power politics, the willful blindness that allows twenty

percent of the world's population to suffer miserably of malnutrition and preventable diseases; these are negative creations. These cultures and mindsets are shared by large populations. They are all creations produced by those groups. The negativity feeds on itself.

Des: Just what large populations do you mean?

Val: There are lots of people out there pointing fingers at other people, and even trying to change them, Des. But very few try to change themselves.

Des: Could you give me a more direct answer?

Val: People are people wherever they live, and whatever they do. Given any set of circumstances, they all react pretty much the same.

Christmas Day, 2007 At Val's Grave

This evening just before dark I walked down to the cemetery just around the corner to Val's grave. I had been bid to do so. Then I wandered around the old section and looked at the dismal, rain-soaked wreckages that remained of some of the graves. There were no flowers in sight. Probably they were not visited for generations.

Is that all we are? Here in physical for a few heartbeats and then forgotten? There was a heavy feeling within me. On the way home I stopped by her grave again.

There she gave me a hug, and I knew with a strange emotional intensity, that in spirit, the group is a warm, living, nurturing organism. The sometimes desperate loneliness that is part of separation and isolation is restricted to the physical. In physical we are compelled to survive. We are prompted to seek out a reason for it all, and in doing so find some comfort. Its aloneness drives us to find ways of coping with one ever-present fear or another, even if we habitually tend to step around the process. It drives us to search for solace, to create what otherwise would not be created. So we create ourselves, second by second and decade by decade, because of the aloneness we create uniquely.

All this came to me as I stood by the grave in the darkness, strangely warmed and no longer alone. It was almost five months since Val died. A voice said that I could do one of two things. I could either belong to the physical and the world of the abandoned graves, or I could rise above them and dwell on Val's hug and the closeness and presence of a living family. Either way I would create. I could never avoid creating. What I created was up to me.

December 27, 2007
Des: What do you make of my wandering around the cemetery?
Val: Of course it was me who prompted your excursion. There was a reason for it, one that has not occurred to you. You can be prompted by us to do many things, or not do them. You can be provided with philosophical concepts. Conversely your mind can be blanked out briefly and selectively to steer what you receive from us, all with your agreement at one level or another. You have explored these things, sometimes with slight discomfort. What you have not explored is the extent to which emotions are an important part of the conduit. On Christmas Day the opportunity was taken to comment on several things, but mainly we were exercising the power of the conduit to inform you by means of your emotions.

November 24, 2007 The Environment in Spirit

Des: I'm ranging far and wide again with my questions. Are you aware of a place with houses and trees? Can you actually define the place you're in now?

Val: In this place we are aware of what we are. We are every experience of a physical lifetime. It can be seen that the physical is very, very important and that it makes us what we are. Physicality does not create consciousness, but it enables us to mold our absolute uniqueness out of consciousness. The physical enables us to draw on every action and reaction, every fleeting thought, emotion, dream, fantasy and romantic notion, every beautiful flower, scene and color, because all these things remain within us. They are available to our uniqueness. We are able to clothe ourselves in them, live and be them.

Des: But not the negative stuff, because you don't have the negative emotions to allow those experiences to register

Val: That's right. So I spend my time in beautiful environments devoid of negative energy. One more thing, Des, we all live in a different beautiful place while apart, but we share a common beautiful place that suits everyone when we come together. It just happens.

Des: And your personal place is shaped and given a reality by your physical life experiences?

Val: Yes it is.

VII. The Journey of a Dead Baby

April 4, 2008
I have encountered Tanya and passed the time with her since Val died, but nothing more than a slightly kidding father-daughter exchange took place. The first significant dialogue with her follows.

Des: Hi Honey. Could you give me an account of a typical spirit personality entering physical and then leaving again after a miscarriage or termination as you did?

Tanya: Okay father of mine, here goes. I really am privileged to be included in your project, even if it was me who asked. Free will and all that, you know. Although I'm not aware of doing so, I moved from the highest reaches of spirit, which I was personally capable of achieving, into coarser and coarser matter as I approached the proximity of the physical in order to fuse with the body of Mum. She is here overseeing my contribution.

As I took on increasingly coarse matter I changed, losing the oversights and resources I had achieved. By the time I fused with the physical I was isolated and entrapped. I was able to disengage and re-engage during the time immediately following conception, although this became more difficult as I was captured by the influence of heavy matter. Nothing seemed different until the miscarriage, when I was again in spirit, but in a completely different place.

Des: Because you now carried very heavy vibrations, coarse spiritual matter?

Tanya: Yes, but I don't remember. My awareness was restricted to that of a baby. It felt the same as though physically I was born. I was with people I later learned were members of my inner group or family. There were two separate lots of people, yours and Mum's, but they came together as one where I was involved. They still do. Sometimes there are parts of lots of groups present if there is a common interest, and they all merge as the inner group. Family groups and greater groups are completely fluid; they come together and separate as the circumstances change. It's all driven by love and affinity, but there's always a reason for this merging and parting. My arrival was greeted with excitement and deep love, very much more so than if I'd been born into the physical.

Des: Why would that be, Honey?

Tanya: Our babies and children, at least those belonging to this family, are fairly rare. Also the only people who could be in my proximity as a baby, and even now, for that matter, were those with a bond of love and affinity.

Des: But surely that would include everyone in your environment, in the family group as well as the greater group.

Tanya: Oh yes. But it's not the case where you are. In the family here, anyone who wants to can have the baby for as long as they want. It is a privilege. People cherish the rare opportunity. Everyone has the same love for the baby as the most devoted mother in physical. The baby doesn't actually belong to anyone. The whole group embraces, shares, and nurtures the new arrival; and the child later on. There are none of the stresses present that you find in physical.

Des: You've been talking to your mum about that?

Tanya: Of course. Lots. You know what women are like, Dad! But even before Mum joined us, I was very aware of the physical.

Des: Perhaps we can talk about that a bit later on?

Tanya: Sure. Now is later on. From the time my emotions and intellect grew, I was able to communicate with anyone who wanted to communicate. That was virtually anyone within the family part of the group. As the communicating continued, my personality and experience sort of were shaped by the group, because different people were sharing parts of their physical life with me, their emotions as well. More and more I was becoming a sort of composite of their different lives.

April 5, 2008

Des: I've got a general idea of how it all works, but could you tell me anyway?

Tanya: Consider it done! I communicate with a loved one, a person in the group and more often in the family. Our minds come together. I almost live the mental and emotional activities that my host wants me to experience in physical. I know the other's fears, the way she defends against them, her hopes and goals and dreams, successes and failures, joys and sorrows, and what interpretation she put on the whole lot. I accompany the person on physical journeys, and immerse myself in their emotions and am a part of their wonders. I get the feeling of swimming, and being hot and cold, and walking in the night. Things like that.

Des: What about relationships?

Tanya: Yes, I live the relationship between a parent and children, my host and her parents, my host and somebody she didn't get on with. I have all sorts of emotions. Because people love and hate a particular thing differently, I had a lot of interpretations. People in physical experience one life at a time. They are trapped, locked in, almost suffocated by the experience. That's all they know.

Because I have lived selective parts of lots of lives, I have a different viewpoint. I was never stuck up to my neck in the swamp, knowing that sooner or later I would drown. I was free to visit and then leave. I have tip-toed along the edges of the swamp, before departing to do the same elsewhere. I know what it all feels like in a distilled type of way. I can make comparisons that are not often possible in the physical. All those loved ones have summed up their lives for me. I do have trouble identifying with their awful intensity.

Des: I understand people like your mum, who lived a full physical life, also use the same communicating process.

Tanya: Oh yes. It's part of life here. But where Mum shares experiences with others, I mainly take experiences. She's giving me more details right now. When Mum talks with people, she interprets what they share with her. She sees it in the light of her own physical life. At this time, she is her own physical lifetime. This will continue until she grows away from its influence. But there are other differences between Mum and me.

Des: Is she still as bossy as ever?

Tanya: She's laughing at that. Mum has been reliving her own life in great detail. This is still ongoing. Once she loosens those ties, there are other dimensions to be explored that are extensions of her physical life. She takes quite different stuff from the minds of group members than I do.

Des: Are you aware why you entered physical in the first place? This time around, I mean.

Tanya: No, I don't know that, Dad. I won't know until I distance myself more from the influence of physical.

Des: When that process is complete, and you return to the realm you came from, will you end up in exactly the same place?

Tanya: No, I'll be on a higher plane, spiritually a more complete place.

Des: Because you were in physical?

Tanya: No, because of my presence in the family after returning to spirit. I'm benefiting from all that learning.

Des: Is the higher plane you came from higher than the place your mum came from?

Tanya: I don't know things like that.

Des: Are you benefiting from this communication with me?

Tanya: Oh yes!

Des: Are you looking forward to progressing spiritually?

Tanya: Yes, yes, yes! It's incredibly exciting. I'm expanding my awareness all the time. It's as though nothing else matters.

Des: But you're happy where you are?

Tanya: I'm as happy as it's possible to be. There's nothing else here except happy. As we move further away from the physical, our ability to experience positive emotions increases. Joy, love, fulfillment and creativity, even emotions that have no meaning in physical, all grow within us. It starts, Mum is saying, from shortly after physical death. The process never stops. She says that the physical is almost an unnatural state, existing in isolation, crushing all within it. It was created to create what otherwise would not be created.

Des: Something I've wondered, what are your emotions compared with your mum's?

Tanya: Compared with how she was in physical, she feels a peace and completeness she can barely relate to. Compared with me, Mum is still battered and bleeding and terrified. That's what her emotions feel like to me.

Des: Compared with other people in the greater group, how does Mum come across? Who or what is she?

Tanya: Mum is very unusual. Within her is an intense light. Even in the physical she did work that was special. But you already know about that. She has responsibilities to the Organism that extend beyond her own growth. In the group we are all much more because of her presence.

Des: Are you proud of her?

Tanya: Oh yes. Completely!

Des: Can you tell me about the evolved personalities, the Beings of Light, I have discussed with my guidance?

Tanya: Yes.

Des: How are they different?

Tanya: Well, they have developed love, empowerment and knowledge in a way that nobody else has. They are able to guide the total human family. We love and respect them.

Des: They don't belong to any particular group?

Tanya: Oh no. They represent the Organism, every group added together.

Des: Do they communicate with people the same way you do?

Tanya: No. They are influenced by different natural laws. They communicate with every group, sometimes at once. They talk to everyone when they want to. We can feel their presence and their emotions. They inspire us.

Des: Do you have any advice for me, Honey? Is there anything I need to know but don't know?

My question was greeted with silence. Then Tanya said "No", gave me a goodbye hug and departed. But something was being kept from me, something lying in the future. I could feel it. I have spent a lot of time with Daughter, most of it when she was eleven, and I could feel her emotions.

VIII. Does a Spirit Even Exist?

November 29, 2007

Des: I understand that one's higher self is the part of us that puts experiences of one type or another in our path during our physical journey, even on a day-to-day basis. That way we are guided in the physical, according to an overriding agenda best known to our higher self. But our free will is just that, free, and represents the final arbiter so far as our behavior is concerned. Is that how you see it?

Val: No it's not. Each of us is a oneness. We can put different names to different parts of that oneness; soul, spirit, the physical or whatever, but as with your physical body, the bits are joined into a single, individual organism.

   Natural law dictates that you learn what you entered physical to learn. Natural law, not your soul, brings in the lessons. There seems to be no soul, higher self or spirit, if we think of them as separate bodies. We are not like islands in a river. We are like the river itself. I see the physical as a perspective of spirit.

Yes Des, a place of suffering, but more as a state where we are isolated from one another in the interest of becoming different from one another, and undergoing a forced growth experience.

Des: Would I be right to say that the higher self, the soul and the spirit, *one has to call them something*, are just reference points so we are able to make sense of them, and talk about them. There has to be a common language if we want to compare notes.

Val: We're both using analogies, Des, just slightly different ones. One is not right while the other is wrong. Most of the analogies I use are going to unfold and make understandable more complex issues.

Because you are in physical, and everything seems to be isolated and encapsulated, you tend to project this concept into the after-death state. It's how you think, how you're programmed. Even physical and spirit are one and the same and not separate estates.

Des: Why would my guidance use a particular analogy, knowing you would use a different one?

Val: They presented a simple but broad overview, an explanation that you and I could build on. Mine is the same analogy, just fleshed out. I've provided more detail, and taken it a step further. You had to have that overview before we could build on it.

December 1, 2007 Death: What is it?

Des: I seem to have encountered quite a lot of death recently, including you and Gremlin the cat. Do I have anything in particular to learn, perhaps relating to my physical responsibilities?

Val: Death is part of life, and you have a lot to learn about life. Death is a beginning and an end. Its sharp edge is fear. If one is able to remove all fear of death, the experience can cease to be one of negativity and turns into something else, a rose petal, a smile in a child's eyes, a beautiful lake at sunrise. Surely these things are far removed from terror. With fear and ignorance death is one thing. Without fear, death is something quite different. With the heaven and hell dichotomy of the Church, death can be an unknown journey, a fearsome balancing act underpinned with guilt. One thing we seek to do with this book is make a start at changing the perception of death, and therefore of life itself, and also to encourage others to do the same. Yes, your role in the physical is being furthered.

Des: I guess the terror-death link is there for a reason. It was created out of consciousness by the Organism, because it served a need for a large number of people. It is part of that overall belief structure that was created to meet a need. In other words, tormented though it may seem, it is perfect.

Val: Certainly, otherwise it would not have been given form and reality. Growth means being adaptive. Humanity stands on shifting ground. The somewhat brutish tendencies of people over several thousand years, with many exceptions, are being replaced. No longer is raw fear so necessary in teaching the lessons of life. Now there is a greater sensitivity. A new order is gaining momentum. We are part of that.

Des: Perhaps fear of death, nevertheless, continues to have a necessary function.

Val: Tell me.

Des: Well, surely we need a powerful emotional incentive to remain in the physical, what literally is hell. Otherwise some people might be inclined to take their leave.
Val: With a dawning understanding of the role of the physical and its absolute significance, which even you don't seem to grasp fully, people are going to value the gift that every second in physical represents. You should give this matter more thought.
Des: You're still bossy.

December 21, 2007 Two Friends Die Together
Des: I've been weighing up a whole raft of unrelated issues here. Let's say two friends die together in a motorcycle accident. Would they continue to keep each other company immediately after death? What about the longer term?
Val: I take it you mean bosom buddies with a real relationship and genuine affinity. The precise nature of their interface before death would dictate the precise nature of their interface after death. In the immediate after-death state their proximity one to another would be more significant than later on, because it would be more exclusive. They would probably be the only ones there. If their bond before the accident were superficial, in all likelihood each would find himself completely alone.

After the initial period a whole lot of relationships unfold in their respective groups. The two good friends come together as part of that, because they represent a joining of the two groups. If they belonged to the same group in spirit, there would be no coming together of two groups. In the longer term, more powerful family relationships would override, and claim the interest and attention of both.

December 28, 2007 No Coincidences?
Des: Okay, were you born at a particular time to do certain things? Did you leave the physical exactly as and when planned? Is it the same for everyone, such as Benezir Buttho who was assassinated in Pakistan last night?
Val: Yes Des, it is the same for everyone. Things happen at a certain time for a reason. As you know, people like you and I have responsibilities in the physical, and by extension, in spirit to follow. But the same principle applies to all.
Des: Is every moment arranged along these orderly and inevitable lines?
Val: Actually it's quite complicated. Energy seeks expression in certain ways in order to unfold potential and learning in an orderly manner. We are all part of this dynamic, in spirit and in physical. *Natural law treats every human being differently from every other, a very important consideration.* By extension this exclusiveness includes the family and greater group in spirit, reinforcing each group's identity while ensuring its unique agenda for growth.

Every person and group in spirit, and every person and gathering of people with a common interest in physical, of whatever size but occupying common emotional ground, is treated differently by the same natural law.
Des: All rather strange!
Val: In simple terms, let's just say that different people and different congregations of people have different valid needs as far as their unfoldment is concerned.

Des: It's a bit like my falling off the roof faster than the neighbor falls off his roof.

Val: Natural law is able to accommodate the valid needs of people across a spectrum of different circumstances. The speed of falling off the roof is not valid or meaningful so far as spiritual unfoldment goes.

Des: The valid needs, I get that. But when you talk about groups of people in physical, does that include ethnic groups and religious groups and family groups, or what? I know. I'm being picky.

Val: Groups within groups within groups. We are talking about common ground linking the people in various groups into fluid and merging mental, emotional and physical environments. Also events overtaking people and groups of people in physical influence the way in which natural law relates to those people. This is due to the fact that everything defers to individual and collective free will. Because people drive events with their free will, they influence the way natural law relates to them as they change from one activity to another, from one event to another. One event may involve a family greeting the birth of a baby. Another may involve soldiers involved in internecine warfare. The two groups will behave quite differently. At a particular point in time one of those soldiers may be present in the family group greeting his new baby. Natural law would treat the soldier quite differently as he moves from one environment to another, because his valid needs change as they relate to his spiritual unfoldment.

To refocus on the question about coincidences, everything happens at a certain time for a certain reason, to every human being within the Organism. The manner in which this process plays itself out is different for every individual.

December 31, 2007 Free Will

Des: Let's say that Mary suffered from depression and John drank too much alcohol. Their relationship in physical was far from perfect. Was their relationship rocky because this was intended by both of them?

Val: No. I'm aware that some information I give you tends to differ from what you believe, but mainly this is because you are replacing existing models with ones containing more detail. Because this makes them more comprehensive, it alters the shape of the model.

Everything defers to free will. We can agree there. But just how we use our free will in physical is influenced by different factors. Namely our personal spiritual resources, which can be mature or modest, the options made available to us by our culture, genetic makeup, modeling from our parents, prevailing events in the environment, and so on. These things dictate the boundaries within which we can function. But within those boundaries free will is the final arbiter, free will has the final say. This is so collectively and at the individual level. Mary's free will, exercised within the limitations of her health problems, shapes her life and her future, and in some measure that of the people with her. The same with John. There is a reason why this couple saddled themselves with depression and alcohol, a situation they carefully put in place at one level or another. The lessons they sought were made available by the suffering and various coping mechanisms that were part of this particular growth environment. How they coped, and how this affected their relationship, was a matter for their respective free wills.

January 8, 2008 Behavior Affecting the Physical

Des: Armed with this all-powerful free will, what are we doing wrong in the physical, and what are the implications?

Val: You might ask what are we doing right. Where one person hurts another or ignores his valid needs, a fundamental natural law is broken. For the moment let's forget about excuses and reasons. There will always be a reason for discriminating against another person if one's heart is so inclined. Where natural law is contravened, invariably there will be consequences. There must be consequences for hurting others, or even ignoring their plight. The consequences vary at the individual level. Collectively the picture is clearer. In extreme circumstances over time the emotional environment changes, and with it the intellectual and then the physical environment. This eventually has an influence at every level down to the individual. The effects then flow on to spirit as people die and behavior is modified.

Where storms, earthquakes and other violent phenomena are encountered partly as a result of our behavior, it is tempting to see these inevitable events within the planetary organism as punishment. They should be seen as learning, unfoldment, going forward.

Des: I guess our habit of destroying our physical environment is not exactly conceptive either.

Val: Violence against the planet and its flora and fauna and its other balances breaks natural law as well. It's like a person cutting off his hands or feet.

January 10, 2007 Prophecy

Des: What do you make of the predictions or prophecies of people like Edgar Cayce, Mother Shipton and Nostradamus?

Val: Actually there's nothing too complicated about this phenomenon. Energy comes into it because energy comes into everything. In the case of Edgar Cayce, he plugged into the energy source you know as the common subconscious mind. But that term means nothing in itself. To look into the future, although he did much more than this, Cayce became receptive to a process that was made available to him because of the role in life to which he was born. Events from the future, lifted from the fabric of consciousness, were given to him to examine.

Des: By whom, or by which agency?

Val: Natural law. No further details are available to the analogies we have at this particular time. Because of Cayce's efforts, natural law was able to balance the growth process as required. The physical community benefited from being aware of certain currents, possibilities, potentials and perspectives, not necessarily what would happen in the future. In the process the needs of the community were being met. People were enticed, inspired, excited and extended. They were encouraged to lift their eyes to the stars. People like Cayce, directly and indirectly, contributed to this march forward.

IX. Many Mysteries

November 14, 2007
Des: What do you make of Jesus?
Val: A fairly open-ended question. We all create. Consciousness is the act of creating at every level, and the means to do so. Furthermore we create according to our needs, individually as well as collectively. Those needs sometimes lead us to create a figure or a concept to guide us. We are steered by our own hand, unfold ourselves, contribute to the orderly growth of our species.

Des, you have been wondering whether or not that makes him real. He is real because he was created. He had a mother and father. He was born, performed various deeds and died. He continues to exist in spirit as part of the Human Organism. Whether he should be deferred to or even worshipped is a matter for free will and the law of individualization, not a matter of right or wrong. You have another question.

Des: Is he real in the same way ordinary people are real? Were we all created because of collective need? If not, what is the difference?

Val: Consciousness largely is unknowable, functioning as it does through mysterious webs of natural law. There have been people and groups appearing in physical throughout history due to the demands of collective growth rather than individual growth. Teachers like Jesus make an appearance. Growth is shepherded. It should be remembered that there are as many ways of responding to natural law as there are human beings. Free will is free will, and every person embraces and is part of his or her own unique web of natural laws, which is part of that particular eternal journey. This is one indication of the importance of every human being.

Des: Somehow I feel a little unsatisfied by this answer. It seems incomplete.

Val: Not by chance. You must complete the answer, because in doing so you are completing yourself, or at least contributing to the process. This is one role Jesus had in his life in physical, and continues to have. By means of this process he is still creating at the physical level.

December 10, 2007 Aliens or UFOs

Des: From one mystery to another. What do you know about the phenomenon we refer to as aliens or UFOs?

Val: Think of a river. It has many streams draining into it as it meanders across the landscape toward the sea. The sea has many rivers emptying into it, big and small, from many countries. One of those small rivers is the human race. Another river is another race. Consciousness, the infinite matrix, is the sea that joins them all, and provides evaporation and rain to nurture the many landscapes. The air and the soil are consciousness. There are planets, galaxies and star systems. They also are consciousness, part and parcel of a great oneness, extending for all time into the past and the future. Of all the alien varieties of advanced life, none have any concept of physical form as we know it.

Des: An evaluation, I guess, which must be a hypothetical generalization, and obviously an analogy at that.

Val: Certainly.

January 6, 2008 The Famous Kennedy Family

Des: I've been watching a television documentary on Jackie Kennedy. She died some time ago, as did her son, husband President John F. Kennedy, brother-in-law Robert and other family members. In spirit the clan undoubtedly is together, and possibly involved in a project of one type or another. Do you have any details? I guess they are still Roman Catholics?

Val: They share a common religious belief. They belong to the same group and the same small part of it. They share the same interests and preoccupations that bound them in physical.

Des: Presumably their total group consciousness is aware that their religious faith is not exclusive so far as right and wrong. How could they continue to embrace Catholicism while also acknowledging the validity of atheism and agnosticism and humanism, even the Eastern religions?

Val: Because they choose to. They continue to create within themselves what they choose to create as a free-will decision. In deferring to a more liberal model they create it within themselves. Individual and shared beliefs vary within any group and even within inner groups, as individuals learn, change and mature. Even before their respective deaths, it is safe to say that different members of the family held to slightly different religious interpretations.

Des: I can see that, but can you expand on it?

Val: The energy that a family group shares and is part of, radiates into other areas and carries with it emotional messages that they seek to broadcast.

Des: What areas?

Val: Well, the common subconscious mind is an example. This is accessed by everyone in physical. Spirit directs emotional and other energy into this reservoir that is tapped by those with similar views. This becomes part of growth and individualization, contributing to cycles. The more evolved a spirit personality, the more enablement his contribution carries. Individuals representing the Organism itself are able to qualify entire areas, but this process always defers to free will at the physical level.

Different family groups radiate slightly different messages. Opposing messages even can be broadcast by these groups, tending to reinforce or cancel one another. The greater group representing a consensus similarly contributes, as do congregations of greater groups that have their own identity. The Kennedy family shares a particular preoccupation in shaping and broadcasting energy in this way. Their primary interest is not concerned with their faith, but rather is focused on broad humanitarian issues affecting the planet.

January 14, 2008 Abortion

Des: I know the Kennedys had strong views on abortion. What do you think about abortion?

Val: The exercise of free will, including the process of making decisions and accepting responsibility for them, is a principal reason for life in the physical. Of course a termination may involve a whole string of free-will decisions on the part of a number of people. Some are influenced by the immediate and extended family, social culture, and religious or philosophical attitudes, as well as the rights of both parents. There is no right or wrong, apart from hurting oneself or hurting another person. There are merely different viewpoints or perspectives, each driven by individual needs. We all have different needs to meet, so we choose different options. The question of abortion comes into this. It is neither right nor wrong. The decision helps to create the individual making the decision.

Abortion is tied intimately into collective preoccupations as well. Groups of people tend to have a strong and unwavering emotional investment in the case for abortion or against it, with only a scant interest in the opposing point of view. Conflict and growth are inevitable.

January 15, 2008 A Killer and His Victim: Their Roles

Des: I read recently in a magazine of a young woman who apparently was murdered in 1960. Did the twenty-year-old choose before she was born, to be murdered? Did the killer choose to kill her, even before he was born?

Val: It must be accepted Des that the more complex a situation, such as the one surrounding this woman, the more simplified has to be any explanation if you are going to be able to receive it. A river is riven with currents and eddies. Some sections of the river, forced from the surface to the bottom and vice versa, cascading over rocks, moving into deep and brooding holes beside the bank, move with great speed. Bring to mind two adventurous swimmers in the river. They are swept one way and another at the mercy of the currents. So it was with the woman and her killer. Because of the exercise of their free will, both entered the river and were swept downstream together. They elected to enter a particular environment for their own reasons and face the perils existing there.

Des: What would their reasons be? How would their spirit minds come into this?

Val: Their spirits' agenda in physical included goals and lesser lessons to be learned. These were shaped by tendencies flowing from past lives, feeding future resources according to the maturity of the spirit itself. They were shaped by physical influences such as their respective genetic pool, upbringing and social circumstances.

During the brief and brutal events which marked this particular meeting, all these factors came together. A desperately forced learning experience was entered into by each of them; much of it was destined to be played out in spirit.

Des: I've been told that there is no such thing as an accident or a coincidence. Yet these people were carried downstream and swept one way and then another with no personal control.

Val: Let's look at what we mean when we say there is no accident or coincidence. From a God's-eye view, from the highest perspective, a person's physical life can be seen like a ruler. One end is birth. The other end is death. Every event and decision that takes place throughout life can be seen happening. Trains of cause and effect are recognized. These occurrences are guided by the unerring hand of natural law, and in the process each individual is enfolded in a unique web of balance, enablement and influences which feeds back and moves forward in time. There is no time, so there can be no such a thing as an accident or coincidence. Remember, this is a Gods-eye view.

Less can be discerned from a less elevated spiritual viewpoint. The oversight becomes limited. From a perspective only slightly removed from heavy matter, and from physical itself, whole areas are obscured and foreclosed. It appears that everything happens by random chance, and you are likely to be in the wrong place at the wrong time.

X. Personalities in Spirit

January 12, 2008

Des: I've been glancing back at my notes of our discussions shortly after you died, more precisely at the brief mention of your first encounters with your parents, and then Tanya and O'Shira. Can you give me any further details, whatever you feel is appropriate?

Val: There was an increasing lightness, emotional warmth, and a sense of being included. The feeling of aloneness was gone completely. But it seemed as though some time passed before that resolved into a more complete awareness of being with Mum and Dad. I was a bit surprised they were together, given their unhappy relationship. Later I learned that their antagonism truly had drained by then. I knew that one can flick from one family interface to another with a thought. They could have been with their own family groups, but appeared together to greet me.

    I integrated more and more into family life and met other family members. We shared experiences directly. Unlike the physical, there was none of the discomfort, reluctance or embarrassment that can be caused by fear of being judged or rejected.

Now to young Tanya. I can't understand how, in physical, I felt removed from her as though she were merely a concept rather than a person. Because I am detached from much of the negative physical energy, I have come to know her much better than I know Quentin or Mel, whom I love very much. But with Tanya I'm aware that she is excited by my presence and enjoys being with me. As one person gets to know another person better, positive bonds increase and the relationship becomes more significant.

I met O'Shira, this spiritual mentor, whom I used to channel, some time after meeting the family. He is wise, gentle, loving and a very significant part of the Human Organism that is dedicated to steering and enabling consciousness at the physical level. In one way the power of love gains focus in physical because of the intervention of these Beings of Light. Even more than before, I feel privileged to be in their proximity and a little in awe of them.

Des: I understand they are ordinary, if accomplished, human beings. Why be in awe of them?

Val: They are more than that. They seem almost to be a different species. Natural law gives them abilities others don't have, so they can influence events. Their presence transforms any environment. Even while in physical form, positive shifts in consciousness usually are the result of their intervention.

Des: When they're in the physical, is there any way of recognizing them for what they are?

Val: Not by an individual also in physical.

Des: Does their presence not skew the process of free will?

Val: These people exercise their own free will like the rest of us. In the process, among other things, they invite others to acknowledge potential they possess, that is waiting to be acknowledged.

Des: They steer others?

Val: They encourage others to steer themselves.

Des: Both in spirit and physical?

Val: Both in spirit and physical.

Des: Have people like O'Shira always been like that, or have they climbed up the ladder?

Val: Very much the latter. In fact the entire human race is climbing the same evolutionary ladder, in terms of how they express consciousness. It's just that people like O'Shira are a rung higher and therefore guiding the process. Natural law gives them the means to do so.

Des: Some people in physical might refer to them as angels?

Val: And some might call them demons, depending on what they are taught.

Des: So someone like Adolf Hitler one day will stand where O'Shira now stands? As a Being of Light?

Val: Let's say you were once a child in kindergarten, Des. You aren't now. Growth has taken place. There are kids in kindergarten at the moment who might end up with a Nobel peace prize. A four-year-old is no less worthy or divine than a Nobel laureate.

Des: So Hitler is like a four-year-old and O'Shira is like a Nobel laureate. Can you tell me more precisely how someone like O'Shira fits into the functioning of the hierarchy? Does O'Shira originate the information you pass to me?

Val: Oh no. That's not his role. They come from another source.
Des: Who is that?
Val: I don't have a name to give you. The information now comes directly from the source, and is not stepped.
Des: It seems strange that you are given some details and not others. Sometimes you have a wealth of information on a subject, and at other times nothing.
Val: If the answers are appropriate to the agenda of the conduit, they are given to me. If you are able to relate to them and they fall within the boundaries of the language of common concepts you share with spirit, they are given to me. Otherwise I receive nothing and say so.
Des: Is Jesus a Being of Light?
Val: Yes he is.
Des: Is he the source?
Val: No.
Des: O'Shira at least has a name. I can't help wondering why your source has to be such an amorphous presence, why he has to step back so far.
Val: Names are not required where one personality can direct areas of awareness into the mind of another. O'Shira identifies himself with a name only because he works with the physical.
Des: I guess the source is plugged into this conversation?
Val: You've already been told he is, when you ran your questions about him past your guidance before asking. You're not one to take risks, Des!
Des: I guess not. You seem to be amused by this exchange.
Val: Of course.
Des: Goodnight Val.

January 18, 2008 12:10 p.m. Channeling This Book

Des: Leaving aside the undeniable advantages of IADC®, it interests me that most other people don't seem able to bridge the gap between physical and spirit.

Val: We've both communicated with spirit since we were young. Over the decades a language of concepts, common to physical and spirit, has been built up and expanded. Spirit has driven this to facilitate communication. The questions and answers exchanged between you and your guidance, over the last twenty-five years especially have been an important part of this process. Tanya was involved as well. The details you were able to receive became more and more comprehensive.

A lot of mediums lack an adequate common language when it comes to linking with spirit, and so are unable to discern details. They receive what they can. Their information can be very general.

Many books containing philosophical information passed on from spirit *(e.g. Neale Donald Walsch, Jane Roberts, Ruth Montgomery, Dr. Ian Gordon)* contain broad and undeveloped models which rely in varying degrees on theories and concepts more or less known to people with an interest in the subject. A particular explanation is picked up and put into writing. With additional detail received, not only is the account from spirit fleshed out, but also a quite different and much more comprehensive description is available. The books in question contain accounts from spirit that discuss a particular reality. With the availability of more detail, a totally different reality is described, because more adequate analogies are present to unfold the descriptions.

In your case you also benefit from the enablement which the source makes available, because of his direct involvement within the conduit. He provides a focused energy that otherwise would not be present. Finally there is the neuropsychological trance that you use, IADC®, a very significant contribution in itself.

January 18, 2008 5:20 p.m. Does God Answer Prayers?
Des: Let's really put the conduit to the test! Can you tell me whether God answers prayers? If so, how and why?
Val: The answer is no if we see God as a concept separate from the figure which belongs to one religion or another, for instance Jesus, Buddha or Muhammad. A useful definition has it that God is the totality of energy, the totality of consciousness, and also what gives rise to it. In a different way, God is a symbol to give people an identity, and a sense of meaning about their role in life. People have always concocted a god to meet their needs. Although they don't use the same term, atheists and agnostics also hold to one godly principle or another so they can define themselves. A billionaire may worship money or material possessions. A politician may worship at the altar of some abstract political notion. An existentialist may defer to an idea that he interprets so it meets his needs. Then he wraps it around himself as though to keep warm.

There is nothing wrong with all this. But you can see how every single individual creates something different, because every individual has different needs to meet.

There are as many gods as there are people. Decide which god you are asking about, Des.

To refocus, if you pray to God for help, you are praying to yourself. You are likely to grant it providing the prayer to yourself meets the agenda of your eternal soul. If John Smith prays he will win Lotto, his request probably does not represent what he came to physical life to achieve. He is challenging the aims of his spiritual being. His prayers will not be answered.

XI. Jesus and Hitler: Their Relationship

February 3, 2008

Des: During a recent discussion you suggested that luminaries like Jesus, Buddha, Muhammad, Confucius and Zoroaster were no different from ordinary people. I don't quite follow.

VAL: We didn't say that, Des. We said that no person is more important than any other. A spirit personality dwelling in the upper reaches of the human condition invariably has unfolded more growth than a killer who recently died. The mature spirit or Being of Light, with overriding responsibilities and corresponding resources, expresses consciousness in a more aware manner. He is an adult and not a child in spiritual terms. Adolf Hitler is a child.

Des: Hypothetically Jesus would feel the need to console and guide Hitler?

VAL: Certainly. And his many victims. All are products of the physical experience and have undergone the consequences of individual and collective free will. All have suffered at the hands of the process called trial and error, the only way in which learning can take place.

Des: Hitler as well?

VAL: Surely. Hitler's emotions and principles were formed and put in place before he was an adolescent, largely before he started school. You can't blame a five-year-old.

Des: The adult must be held accountable.

VAL: We agree. Perhaps it is easier to hold him accountable than to judge him. Just make sure you know who it is you judge.

Des: I'm not sure the Church would give me many brownie points for associating Jesus with Hitler!

VAL: Jesus is an evolved personality, a Being of Light, whether we are talking about spirit or physical. On Earth his spirit was clothed in a normal physical body. He was gentle and loving, a healer and a teacher. He was not the bigoted and intolerant deity sometimes painted by the Church, demanding blood if anyone disagreed with him.

But the real Jesus, the human being, was a normal and unremarkable individual. Many before and after him have been more loving, generous and intelligent. Nothing can deny the fact that Jesus the man was an evolved spirit serving the aspirations of the Human Organism.

Des: And Hitler? Spiritually he was just a child?

VAL: Just a child, a very young one with many lessons to learn and many more mistakes to make. You sound unconvinced. A normal preschooler is capable of being a dictator, self-centered, blindly angry, vindictive and manipulative, completely amoral. There is nothing wrong with that, because a child is a child. He hasn't learned to behave in any other way. He can be endearing and loving as well, but usually on his terms.

Des: Okay, although I'm tempted to say that there aren't many little ones who would maul you to death if you turned your back on them. I acknowledge the principles you've outlined.

At this point I felt ill, and had to discontinue the session. Before doing so I was informed that my discussion about Jesus and Hitler had not involved Val as the intermediary. I had been communicating directly with the source, the personality who previously had been stepped through Val. At one level I was aware of this. When I asked the evolved personality who he was or what I was supposed to call him, he seemed disinterested. I said I'd refer to him as "A". *In retrospect, it occurred to me that something of the resentment or antipathy which I felt occasionally about O'Shira, lingered at this time.*

February 4, 2008

Des: I understand last evening the source was talking to me directly. This made me sick. Who are you?

A: Even now you feel a sense of my more complete control. I can convey details which would be difficult or impossible if I used Val or your guidance as an intermediary. Because it is possible for us to pass information to you directly, there is little reason to use an indirect process.

Des: Why didn't you warn me you would be stepping around Val?

A: We did, Des. Emotionally you were aware that we had started to shade in, even if you were reluctant to acknowledge it.

Des: Is it possible for Val to become resentful, as though she's been sidelined?

A: Not in the case of a mature and significant personality like Val, even though she is still in the shadow of her physical journey. She remains a part of the conduit but in a slightly less direct context.

Des: Was the subject under discussion yesterday the reason why you shaded in and Val shaded out?

A: In part. You won't get a subject emotionally much more loaded than the one we discussed.

Des: You will admit that I was prompted in that direction?

A: Certainly. It is our agenda you are being cued to deliver, not your own. You have been guided throughout your life. You have always been part of this project.

Des: Always?

A: Let's refocus on the subject of Jesus and Hitler. This comparison caused violent and aggressive emotions in people dominated by negative energies, those in the lower reaches of spirit as well as in physical, now and in the past. There is no time in real terms. You moved into and experienced some of those collective emotions in a minor way, which made you ill. Even afterwards you were left with fierce negative emotions of your own. Within this environment your wife is just too vulnerable. Of course we protected her.

Des: You never protected me?

A: Being in physical you are well equipped to deal with negative energies.

Des: Okay, but I thought Val was beyond the reach of negative energy. Why did she need protecting?

A: She remains in the proximity of heavy matter. We are talking here about intense, cumulative emotions on the part of millions of people.

Des: Will I be working with her again?

A: Not directly. You and your wife will communicate and enjoy each other's company whenever you want. The main consideration is your time and energy.

Des: Thank you. You said Beings of Light like Jesus were almost a different life form from lesser ones, although no person was more important than any other. What did you mean?

A: An evolved personality has unfolded a spectrum of resources that a less significant one does not have. It is a bit like you having twenty senses instead of merely six. This provides not only intellectual and emotional advantages, but also a gentleness, capacity for love, and a deep understanding of what others undergo. You have a compelling need to provide guidance, uplift, inspire, heal and nurture the human condition.

The more mature and realized a personality, the greater are these qualities. As you have discussed with your guidance, there are many degrees of unfoldment just as there are many ages and sizes of children. In spirit, the presence of evolvement can be felt as a source of warmth on a cold day, but a warmth that bathes all the senses.

After "A" broke off contact, I caught up with Val briefly. She was relaxed, comfortable and happy.

February 5, 2008

Des: We were discussing a parallel between Jesus and Adolf Hitler.

A: The total Human Organism, containing spirit and physical, produces in an orderly and balanced way what is needed for growth to take place at individual and collective levels.

Take the case of the man who was renamed by history more than once, as Jesus. The demands of collective growth effectively said, "I need a figure who can act as a role model, someone who can inspire and lead, who acts to bring people together." The total Organism produced, out of consciousness and its natural laws, such a person. He lived and died. Fanciful myths were woven and elaborated upon around him. These completely altered the message which Jesus carried. The Christian religion came into being founded on these myths. It must be acknowledged that the fanciful elaborations, which largely were shaped from past religions, tended to reflect the compelling needs of the day. They gained expression within consciousness and were created.

Des: Presumably a certain threshold of need was required, a given emotional intensity plus the required number of people?

A: It's much more complex than that, Des. Patterns existing beyond the immediate environment were involved. We must hold our focus.

Hitler surely was a much less developed expression of consciousness. The appearance of Jesus created positive energy. The appearance of Hitler and his kind did the opposite. They channeled negative energy into the populations affected, negative emotions and behavior of the grossest order. Those negative appetites already existed within the communities of Europe. Hitler merely gave them a vehicle. He was the creation of those who nurtured hatred and fostered discrimination. He represented them.

Des: So we can say that Hitler took to himself the intolerance and viciousness that was part of European society at the time. It became a part of him. After he grew to adulthood he poured it back over them.

A: Yes. Individuals and communities who experience pain are able to understand pain in others, and respond more supportively to it. A quality is born which did not exist before. Negative cycles tend to decay and produce positive cycles, especially in the longer term. Growth, the inevitable consequence of every human activity, is served.

War in Europe and the Pacific produced the environment for this to take place. It was ordered up by the populations affected, in a harsh manner but no more harsh than necessary. They were the ones who caused it, who benefited by their own hand. They produced Hitler and others like him to do their bidding, to heal them, act on their behalf, unfold positive qualities that did not exist.

February 6, 2008

Des: If Hitler was born into physical for a conceptive reason, is it appropriate to condemn him as evil?

A: The answer is yes. He was the embodiment of evil. More to the point, it was community evil that made his appearance appropriate, namely the widespread negativity, even in a more distilled form, that moved beneath the surface of various societies in the years and decades before he made his appearance.

Des: If there is no time could the atrocities of World War II somehow have fed back to the time before the war and contributed to the rise of Hitler?

A: This is what happened. Now we are moving the focus from where we want it to be. As you are aware, Des, you were mildly taken to task by your guidance for telling a client, during a philosophical discussion, that Hitler clearly was a monster. You were using Hitler as an example of emotional polarization.

Des: That's right.

A: Whether or not he was a monster, the important consideration is that he was the product of human frailties. It was a bit much to dismiss him as a monster when your forebears manufactured him. There is a final lesson that Hitler offers to the world all these years after his downfall. Instead of judging him, the physical communities could well look for their own face on his shoulders!

February 7, 2008 The Inevitability of Suffering

Des: Grossly negative behavior in the physical created the likes of Hitler as part of natural law. Have we grown since that time to avoid a similar catastrophe? You seem to be saying no.

A: While the privileged members of society often grow unhealthy through overeating, and waste much of the food they are unable to eat, people from other countries die miserably of malnutrition and preventable diseases by hundreds of thousands.

Des: Many also die in wars among their own tribal groups.
A: I am talking about countries courting another catastrophe. You asked the question. Now ask yourself if civilization should be held accountable.
Des: I suppose so.
A: This behavior proves that a very large amount of growth surely has to come to the developed countries. Suffering is required for this to happen. That is how human nature works. You will suffer in the physical.
Des: How and when?
A: Ask yourself which of many possible futures you are talking about. Collective free will is going to usher in what is necessary.
Des: Okay.
A: There are other aspects of negative behavior making suffering inevitable. One is the inclination to engage in religious conflict. In a worst-case scenario, the destruction of people to prove whose God is better, or right. Carnage in the name of God! Justice must be dealt a hand!
Des: What is likely to happen?
A: You know what is likely to happen if you light fires in dry grass during a swirling gale.
Des: Everyone is likely to be consumed in the fire.
A: Do not forget who has been lighting the fires.
Des: I haven't read about any holy crusades lately.
A: Have you not!

XII. Looking at the Face of God

February 10, 2008 12:30 a.m.

A: For the moment we will look at the face of God. Let us draw a circle and call that circle the Human Organism, the total human experience. Now draw another circle twice as large around it. We are talking about spiritual concepts, or pure energy. The larger circle also is an Organism, actually a living being that exists as part of the process of consciousness. The larger and very much more advanced life form has created the Human Organism as part of itself, and given it a separate identity and destiny. The mind of the more advanced being has projected something that did not exist, given it free will and its own infinite potential.

Let us now draw a larger circle around the two already in place. The largest circle, an even more advanced life form, has created the middle-sized one that created the smallest one, called humanity. The largest circle has created the two smaller ones. This process represents the nature of consciousness. This process of one Being creating another within itself goes on infinitely in an infinite universe.

Des: I guess we are talking about a single Being.

A: No we are not.

Des: How do you know?

A: This is a subject we will touch on later.

Des: Okay. But surely there must be some end to the process.

A: There is not. You know that even in physical terms there is no speed, time or distance. At least you accept this premise. There is only consciousness which does not defer to these limitations. The most enlightened Being directly creates everything within its mind, and indirectly creates what the lesser Being creates, and so on.

Des: And you suggest that the total process is what we refer to as God?

A: Not necessarily the God who is acknowledged by religion. We are talking about the ultimate reality, consciousness. Within consciousness a number of people on the physical plane will find themselves with a common need that demands to be met. Facilitated by natural law, that group of people will produce the composite creation they need. They will produce a god out of the matrix of consciousness.

Des: Have I got it right? Those infinite shells of consciousness represent the most meaningful definition of God. But within this matrix, human free will creates whatever its most pressing needs demand. If they need a so-called God to support, guide and complete them, then natural law provides this. It will support any need that is driven by a certain level of emotional energy.

A: You have it, Des. Think of your physical body. One part adapts to the needs of another part.

February 10, 2008 8:15 p.m. The Enduring Mystery
A: But there is another factor involved. There is something, possibly a potential of some sort that comes and goes, which is removed from and functions beyond consciousness, while having some guiding relationship to it. The question has been asked whether it drives the creative process. Certainly its identity and meaning are beyond the understanding of the human mind. If the Human Organism could comprehend such things it would cease to be human.
Des: It surprises me that you have details about it.
A: When talking to you, your guidance has referred briefly to this presence as The Entity, a name which owes everything to your personal terminology. In the end the term "god" means nothing more than an attempt to meet your own needs, provide you with roots and an identity so you can make sense of the world and yourself. God means anything you want it to mean.
Des: You might undermine my sense of identity by telling me that!
A: Even as we provide you with a more meaningful sense of identity.

February 11, 2008 The Destiny of Every Human Being
Des: If the Human Organism is part of an infinite continuum, then by definition the Organism must be creating infinitely within its own being.
A: Not necessarily, Des. You'll have to qualify that. After physical death, a spirit progressively moves further from

heavy matter. During this time the spirit relives every experience of the incarnation until it has nothing more to offer, then repeats the process with every possible future that the spirit has lived as part of the same physical journey with every lesson it has to offer. Eventually the spirit navigates among so-called past lives, examining the manner in which experience is utilized, identifying the flow of events and their intricate patterns. The total process is fiercely exciting, profoundly creative, becoming more so as the spirit proceeds.

By now the vast numbers of temporary spirit vehicles have been discarded, and we are talking about the functioning of the eternal soul. This estate is comprised of every second that makes up her being. She reconciles every thought encountered, every sight, taste, sound, action and reaction, every success and failure, omission and commission, dream and regret. She processes every nuance of negativity but takes only the lessons from them. She bathes in every joy she has known, and holds them to herself.

She is complete. This is the ultimate balance. Without the need for further direct growth, there is no need for the stress needed to create growth. She is a Being of perfection and complete serenity and love. The Being is unique. Individuality has flowered. No longer is she a god in embryo, but a god. There are now as many gods as there were human beings. Potential has been realized. At some point each god enters into the same creative process that once produced every individual human being in existence. In this way an infinite cycle of rebirth takes place within the body of the Human

Organism, even as it takes place beyond it and is part of it.

Des: So we're talking about the existence of three separate types of god, the perfected human being, the god created out of consciousness to meet the needs of a group of people in physical, and the god which is consciousness or which drives consciousness.

A: We are, Des.

Des: And all this takes place in a reality that is devoid of time. Fairly clever!

XIII. Different Explanations: Why?

February 13, 2008

Des: You have touched on the ultimate reality. Can you tell me why is it that different books on the subject have been written giving different accounts? All ostensibly come from spirit.

A: If one psychic is able to receive a wealth of detail through his channel, he will put together a more comprehensive explanation than one who is able to receive only sparse or generalized information.

Let us say that psychic AB can receive from spirit one fact out of every billion that is available to human understanding, while psychic CD is able to discern two facts out of every billion. Subconsciously, both people create a picture by fitting together all the facts available. Because CD has twice as much raw material, his picture will be twice as detailed. Des is able to come by five items of information out of every billion. The picture in his mind will be the most intricate and revealing.

The books channeled by these three people will appear to provide quite different explanations because of the way their respective minds splice together the incoming information. There is a reason for this. Each psychic's subconscious mind continues to move the available facts around until a logical pattern falls into place that makes use of all the data. A different databank produces a different perspective or explanation. People do this all the time.

Des: In physical and spirit?

A: Yes. Take your case. The sensory information you extract from your surroundings is brought together in your mind. The mind moves it around, processing and constantly re-interpreting it. Eventually the information takes the form of a meaningful picture that makes sense to you. You relate to this picture. By definition you accept it. You might even write about it. It matters not whether the incoming information originates from the physical environment or from spirit.

A larger databank produces a different explanation, not merely a more detailed one.

It is important to realize, that author AB's perspective which appears in her book is neither right nor wrong. The same with CD's reality. Each book meets the emotional needs of a certain segment of the population. The more sophisticated book will be read by those with a deeper and more informed interest in the subject. A whole spectrum of viewpoints made available over a period of time guides everyone with an interest in the subject. Consciousness creates a need and proceeds to meet that need.

Let us look at the question of why you were able to receive five facts out of every billion, while AB and CD received only one or two. You started receiving information from your wife from the time she died.

This progressively became more detailed. The process was helped by the fact that Valerie was a gifted psychic throughout much of her adult life. Because of your personal bond in physical the link between the two planes was developed to an unusual degree.

After the initial few encounters, many of the details she conveyed to you were channeled into her mind by the spirit beings who originated the information, because she did not have answers. The stepping process was involved. There is no intermediary between the source of the intelligence and you in physical. Val is still a valuable link in the process, but in a different manner.

All the foregoing factors added together give you five facts, instead of one or two out of every billion. The most important consideration of all is the neuropsychological technique you call IADC®, which further increases your receptivity.

February 15, 2008 7:30 p.m. Footwork for this Book

Des: What makes me the exception to the rule, so I am able to bypass the intermediary, whether it's Val or my guidance?

A: You provided a part-answer when you confided in one of your long-term clients, "I think something strange has happened to my head. I know things I shouldn't know. They are there but I've never learned them or even heard of them. I think spirit has a sort of campsite in my head." Actually Des, that was pretty apt. By means of this "campsite," information can be directed to you very much as it was given to your guidance and your wife before being stepped down to you. This process has been made possible because you interacted with your guidance and your deceased daughter Tanya, asking questions and receiving answers. The questions and answers were more detailed as time went by. We have discussed other advantages you possess.

A sort of common language of concepts, an area of common denomination, progressively became established. This enabled more complicated ideas to be conveyed to you. An exponential process was in play, where your store of information built more rapidly.

Des: So I can receive five facts out of a billion instead of one or two.

A: Exactly. The common language contains embedded within it an emotional component, another dealing with principles, and others imparting empathy for those in the community, and a broad sense of responsibility to your various environments. In some ways you carry the attitudes of the individuals in spirit you related to during those decades. We have referred to all this, information plus emotions, as a spiritual campsite in your head. Any concepts you are not familiar with will not be picked up by you. The details will not register adequately in your mind. This happened once or twice when you were working with Val.

Des: Just what is it that happened?

A: Your mind continually tried to interpret the thoughts directed to it. Time and again it moved around the incoming information, connected it to associated areas or to subjects it did know about, changed its perspective and context, and generally tried to relate to it in any way possible. If even a small amount of understanding could be achieved, your mind discerned at least something, and an approximate explanation, was presented to you. Because this situation does not meet the needs of the conduit, the details are blocked. Therefore you get nothing. The information you receive through the conduit is carefully shaped.

Des: The general principle explains why some psychic writers receive only broad details and relatively undeveloped explanations.

A: That is right. However let us have a look at the only time during our interface when you became wary, and this orderly process was in danger of becoming impeded. Obviously you are aware of the details.

February 15, 2008 8:03 p.m. Danger Signals

The following took place in the late 1990s. Details are only general, as I have no notes on the exchange. I was aware for some time that I was gently prompted to ask certain questions that appeared in my mind, and avoid others. The questions that I asked resulted in the information that was provided in reply, and so a picture was formed in my mind. I appeared to be forcefully discouraged from pursuing particular lines of thought. I seemed to be pushed away from certain books that came into my possession and intrigued me. I had difficulty understanding their most basic premises, as though my mind were being blocked.

During this time I was engaged in relatively detailed discussions with my spirit guidance. Their answers always steered and manipulated my growing store of information. This process contributed to what I saw as a carefully-controlled bias. I was receptive to a certain interpretation and less receptive to others. My growing collection of common concepts was being shaped. The answers to my questions from spirit seemed to form into a philosophical framework that had little to do with me.

I was being used! Was I being set up as the channel for a carefully scripted message? Was my free will being taken from me? Who or what was I being turned into? I demanded answers. One particular exchange went like this:

Des: Obviously I am being used!
SG: You are.
Des: These dialogues are part of a broader agenda.
SG: That's entirely correct.
Des: What about my free will? You guys are always on about free will.
SG: At every level you agreed to participate. You will remember discussing the matter with us in 1981, when you agreed to take part in the project. Admittedly you were unaware of the exact details.
Des: That's right.
SG: Nothing has changed.
Des: Nevertheless you might have some devious agenda, for all I know.
SG: It's your responsibility to determine that.
Des: How?
SG: Words are only words. Judge us by our actions. Think how many times we have helped with your clients, provided information you personally did not possess.
Des: Quite a lot over the years, I guess.
SG: We never let you down one single time.
Des: That's right.
SG: We never failed to provide personal help or advice when asked.
Des: I guess not.

SG: We have always asked you to defer to your conscience, your principles, your family and social responsibilities, the interests of your clients, and your common sense.

Des: That's right.

SG: Once or twice we even helped with your health, much to your amazement.

Des: Yes, you did that.

SG: It's completely appropriate that you continue to evaluate the relationship between us. In fact you must do so. It's your responsibility.

Des: Why have you skewed the common language we share? I'm quite unable to receive details from you outside the common language. You've done the whole thing on purpose.

SG: Of course we have. We all defer to the agenda to be served.

Des: Determined by whom?

SG: By the Organism, by the spirit personalities who have ultimate responsibility in these areas. You are part of a conduit. A message is to be conveyed to the physical. A common language has been created over your lifetime to carry the message. It was shaped to do so. Your own life experiences contributed.

Des: The events of my life were shaped to that end?

SG: There is no accident or coincidence. That applies to everyone.

Des: If a quite different message were to be channeled, a different common language would have been fashioned?

SG: Yes, if necessary. That hypothetical common language would include everything that was required and exclude almost everything else. The conduit is the name given by you to the individual in physical, and those in spirit, who are charged with the responsibility for conveying the message.

February 23, 2008 Contemporary World is Courting Disaster

Des: I understand that your all-important message relates to this particular time in history. Is our time that meaningful?

A: Every time in history is meaningful. Let us go back a little bit. The human condition produces cyclic movements within its realm of consciousness. Contained within natural law there is an accelerating movement towards one pole, followed by a pause, then an accelerating movement in the opposite direction. Weather patterns over a long period reflect this phenomenon.

Free will can play a hand here; relatively minor events can tip a cyclic movement in one direction or another. Remember, we are resorting to an analogy. An example can be seen with global climate shifts. Collective free will as it contributes to climate change invariably will create one future or another for the planet. Individual and collective decisions that historically may not be significant in themselves can produce or prevent certain events. Some of these collective futures are irreversible.

One pivotal time is now. Depending on changing circumstances it will continue until about 2020. This cyclic process is an important part of human development, acting as it does to force growth. Stagnation becomes impossible.

Humanity is an organism, as is every individual within it, learning and creating itself by the process of trial and error. There is no other way of learning. Free will is an estate where it must be possible to do right or wrong in terms of natural law. Otherwise there is no free will. Cycles feed cycles. This creative process is the basic building block of human evolution, the evolvement of consciousness at the human level.

Des: So we live or die by our own hand.

A: Well, it is not possible to destroy consciousness. It is possible to temporarily destroy the Human Organism at the physical level. Humanity can destroy its physicality according to how it exercises free will.

Des: What do you think is the greatest threat?

A: There are many. We are concerned about nuclear weapons but also about other potent weapons.

Des: It is tempting to blame extremists for a lot.

A: You should know better than that. Poverty causes extremism. Society causes poverty.

Des: I don't blame them. I was just tempted.

A: If you grievously disadvantage a segment of the population, consume their share of the natural resources, damage their pride, social fabric, independence, health, you force them into survival mode. They no longer have much to lose. They will fight back. You would do the same. It's an adaptive part of human nature that ensures survival.

Most important, the disadvantaged people are quite unable to alter the situation which gives rise to their resentments. Only the more wealthy nations can do that. But these nations have a remedy. They spend billions on armaments to threaten or compete with one another. They consider terrorists need to be guarded against. Generations of disadvantaged people become more disadvantaged. Extremist ideologies thrive.

Ask yourself which countries face their conscience and learn from the opportunities presented to them. In the past have they squandered their energies doing the opposite. They have rewritten history, presenting a picture for future generations that denies wrongdoing and blames someone else. They blame terrorists, the terrorists they created themselves.

Des: This is all pretty simplistic stuff.
A: We are using analogies, because there is nothing else available. People are pretty much all the same. They love, shed tears and get angry. They despair and feel inadequate.
Des: So they try to solve their problems by attacking each other.

February 24, 2008 8:00 a.m.
Des: Please go on.
A: We suspect the time is right for us to refocus what is being discussed. The responsibility is on the developed countries to accept that only they can reverse the cycles. You are now living on borrowed time, taking grave risks in continuing to perpetuate the injustices you have created.
Des: Which is part of the natural process of growth called trial and error that we are in the physical to embrace. So there's nothing wrong with it!
A: It is unfortunate that people insist on reruns of wars, that sort of suffering or something worse. In its implacable way natural law will do what is necessary to balance, compensate and adapt human behavior to

meet its overriding agenda for an orderly unfoldment of growth.

The all important message to be conveyed to the physical is not a single message as much as an oversight of the human situation which has never existed in the past. As the result of these words, people now possess perspectives they have lacked. Their free will has become more enabled. They are capable of accepting a more meaningful level of responsibility for their activities within their environments. There is less excuse.

Des: What if this book fails to get off the runway?
A: If the conduit fails in its objectives, then it will fail because of free will at the physical level. This is what we are talking about.

XIV. The Late Great Human Race

February 24, 2008 9:20 p.m.
Des: So you are saying we might have another large-scale war?
A: The exact nature of what happens will depend on the exact nature of the circumstances that continue to unfold. But something more significant is taking place. You already have a broad idea of the details. As well as the specter of widespread turmoil on the physical plane, a basic change in the very nature of the human race is gathering momentum. Change involves the fact that human behavior alters human emotions. That feeds back into genetic makeup at the individual level, a process which goes on to affect the whole human race in a number of ways right through the entire Organism.

   As the genetic makeup of humanity alters, as its genetic code undergoes a subtle shift in emphasis, the very physiology and psychology of the race is changing. People are starting to change into something different. Something mutant is emerging into focus. Nature's version of self-genetic engineering can be glimpsed.

By its own hand, the Organism and its different parts are being reshaped because of their behavior. This will be registered first on the physical plane, but will flow on to spirit and then the soul itself.

Des: If we're forced to talk about the amount of time involved.

A: There is no time.

Des: What's to stop human beings from no longer being human beings?

A: Nothing! Self-indulgence, intolerance, willful blindness to the suffering of others, is making inescapable a situation where generations of people will grow further removed from what they had been. Of course they would distance themselves from such behavior. This process is a part of natural law.

Des: What happens if human behavior changes?

A: The extent of change will decide how much the mutation progresses.

Des: But why has this not happened during the centuries or millennia gone by?

A: The process is exponential and has taken thousands of years to reach the present threshold. Only now has humankind reached the point where the race can be expected to accept responsibility for its own actions.

Des: Clearly this phenomenon comes from beyond the Human Organism.

A: Yes, the Organism itself comes from beyond, as does everything within it.

Des: So the genetic mutation has already started.

A: It started millennia ago. It has now reached a threshold where a small number of children can be seen growing away from their parents, as far as personality, attitudes and behavior are concerned.

But you talked about this with your guidance, Des, even though details were not discussed. You were shown a picture where your grandfather was standing on the ground beneath the floorboards of your house. Your father was standing just above his head on the floor. You were standing on the roof. Your children were in orbit around the planet. And their children were in deep space. It is an accelerating process.

Des: What if the race does something diabolical and wrecks the planet? What happens to the genetic modification of the survivors?

A: They would just carry on in whatever environment they have left. Natural law will provide a physical plane for as long as necessary. In the event of total destruction, a collective future would unfold that no longer contains a contemporary or present-day physical environment.

Des: I don't follow.

A: There is no time as such, so a physical presence would be used that belongs to some time in the past. Learning would flow from there.

Des: So none of this would happen if we were to respond in a mature and responsible way to the challenges facing us.

A: As we've explained. Remember there is no time. The process would not have been started all those thousands of years ago if your present activities were more caring. Your present behavior fed back in time, and set in motion the mutations that a more mature society would not have made necessary. Good behavior now would never have the whole process going, all those millennia ago. The existing bad behavior ensures it is inevitable. Humanity is evolving by its own hand, mentally, emotionally and spiritually. Further details cannot be discussed.

Des: Because it is too complicated?

A: Well, it falls outside the mandate of this conduit, and therefore your ability to understand the explanation.

Des: There are a lot of questions that remain unanswered on this subject.

A: As there should be.

Des: In one context we're a failed experiment, then. Natural law has shelved us. I guess we've shelved ourselves.

A: Everything is natural law. Natural law shelves nothing. It is perfect.

Des: So why tell me all this?

A: Your communities have the right to know. They have reached a threshold where they can benefit from knowing what they are. Even if they are not likely to prevent the process of mutation, they are entitled to be aware of the consequences of abusing the planetary environment and many of its inhabitants. This they can influence. People in the developed countries have come by the growth and resources where they can at last accept responsibility for running their own household. They will benefit from their achievements. They must also accept the consequences for their failures. This is the price of responsibility.

February 28, 2008 The Common Subconscious Mind

Des: It has been explained to me that the common subconscious mind is another way in which events in physical can be guided from spirit. Would you give me more details please? The common subconscious mind, as I understand it, is that part of the mind of every person in physical which is joined together, a reservoir we all share. Every individual draws on this area of awareness, without being aware of it, and in the process obtains critically pertinent insights and emotions.

A: Good. It contains everything that is within the mind of every person in physical. An individual is able to obtain input from this source, and steer unfoldment by drawing from it what is appropriate for the next stage of growth. Natural law uniquely treats every person differently. One way it does this is to use the common subconscious mind to make available particular areas of awareness and inhibit others.

Des: Why does spirit provide an input into the common subconscious?

A: The spirit personalities representing the Organism feed energy into it according to their agenda, and depending on circumstances in the physical. Growth at the physical level can be shepherded, but always within boundaries put in place by natural law. This should give some indication of the importance of the common subconscious. The entire Human Organism has been shaped and given its destiny, at least indirectly, by events in physical. The raw material for the Organism comes from physical experience. This is processed, reworked, refined and extrapolated endlessly by every individual spirit, and by definition, collectively, all spirits added together.

It should not be surprising that feedback to the physical level, made appropriate by changing events, can be provided as a guiding influence. The common subconscious makes this guidance possible, as one of the influences available to natural law.

XV. A Land of Suffering: The Physical

February 29, 2008
Des: What else is the physical plane? What else is its value? How did it come about?
A: The physical is energy that is in place to do a number of things that cannot be achieved in spirit. The physical isolates people from one another. A physical individual is a spirit temporarily clothed in a body, with a tiny part of awareness locked into a sharp focus on the physical environment. The resulting isolation enables the spirit to build greatly onto its unique individuality. Spiritual growth also is nurtured, and even brutally forced if this is part of the agenda of the spirit. This evolvement cannot happen in the same way in spirit, where an almost constant merging of mind takes place and where negative energy relatively is unknown. During the years of any physical life a vast amount of growth takes place almost instantaneously.

The physical estate was created out of consciousness as part of the human condition. The law of limitation is part of it, forcing every individual and group of individuals to fight for survival of one type or another in a place of limitation, in a place of imprisonment in an uncomfortable and lonely cell called pain.

In physical people must cope and adapt, struggling doggedly with their changing vulnerabilities as the years go by, and come to terms with a parade of conflicts. They must try to make sense of their circumstances. This suffering should teach them to surmount the toxic environment, cast off negative emotions and activities and unfold positive ones.

The physical journey offers every person the opportunity to rise above the emotional swamp and float into the stars. Once achieved, he is free and any further physical presence is no longer necessary.

Whether or not you accept the explanation which follows is up to you Des, but the physical universe as a total package is a part of the collective human mind. Every planet, star and galaxy extending forever is part of human consciousness, just as much as every human being is part of human consciousness.

Des: So if humanity somehow was destroyed or switched off like a light, the physical universe would disappear?

A: The entire infrastructure never would have existed in the first place if this were possible.

Des: The sun and the moon are part of me!

A: Start off by asking what you are. At the most meaningful level you are a conception of your own choosing, an identity you have created out of consciousness. When you have finished with your creation you will be complete. By means of the same type of creative process, the total Human Organism has been given the means to create out of consciousness everything in both physical and spirit.

Des: I'm sorry. It sounds a bit too off the planet for me. How could every human mind added together create the sun and the moon?

A: The Organism is infinitely more than just all minds added together. It is part of a continuum going on without end, in which one level of creation exists within another. By means of this process the Human Organism is given the means and the mandate, without being conscious of it, to create what is necessary for an orderly unfoldment of the species. A physical presence is a bedrock on which everything else stands, as far as humanity is concerned. It is necessary, so it was created. Everything in physical form is part of the same concept made up of intensely focused energy. It is there for a split second and it is there forever. It is there solely to unfold human potential and is part of it.

The same creative agency which shapes and animates humanity and its immediate environment out of energy also shapes and animates the larger physical environment. They are all part of the same sentient process.

March 2, 2008 The Law of Limitation

Des: The law of limitation you mentioned, I suspect we haven't succeeded in casting off too many negative emotions.

A: It is where we are right now. Free will is tied to a dynamic which says that good behavior generally leads to comfortable feelings, while bad behavior leads to uncomfortable feelings. Almost despite itself humanity evolves. Casting off negative emotions is part of that.

It all contributes to polarization which is fundamental to physical life. Molecular structure itself relies on polarization. The planet has poles, the North Pole and the South Pole. Gender is polarized into male and female. Religion contains polarized concepts, good and bad, God and Satan, the faithful and the unbeliever, right and wrong, God-fearing and humanist. Democracy by definition is a polarizing force, as are its variants and alternatives. Even God himself gives rise to polarization, as with the long-time divide between Muslim and Christian. It is all polarization. Polarizing behavior is encountered only in the physical, made inevitable by the tensions and conflicts ordered up by the law of limitation.

Let us look at a representative example where free will, polarization and the law of limitation can be seen coming together, the sexual experience. The fierce emotional and physical appetites of flesh propel people in one direction and then another, like tennis balls during a game. Sexuality stokes the fires of competition, possessiveness, jealousy, self-indulgence or hedonism, and provides the opportunity for positive modes of expression. Normal parenting instincts come into this.

Emotional adolescent behavior naturally emerges, during a particularly sensitive part of a young person's life. Status and self-esteem are shaped in the process, especially when one is judged by peers to be undesirable. Sexual orientation is a minefield. Sexual aberrations, violence, victimization and discrimination represent a cauldron of conflict and intense negative emotions. Propagation does not need such a complex and divisive apparatus as sexuality. Evolvement and individualization do. Free will and polarization, driven by the law of limitation, are dealt cards in the game. So it is that the species continues to evolve.

XVI. Prophecy in Detail

March 13, 2008

Des: How is this process of evolvement affected by prophecy? What is its usefulness?

A: As we create at the individual level, so we create at the collective level. Individual free will comes together into collective free will. The future is shaped accordingly. This outcome can be foreseen up to a point by people like Nostradamus, who are in the physical at a particular time equipped with certain abilities and responsibilities.

Des: Presumably the vagaries of human nature mean that a future that has been foreseen can be skewed and changed with the passage of time.

A: Predictions become inexact in various ways. That is right.

Des: What is the use of prophecy in the grand scheme?

A: A situation is created in physical where people are prompted to think about the prophecy, make judgments at a semi-philosophical level, and generally individualize along these lines. Speculation is fostered. Theories are encouraged. Polarization is made inevitable. An environment is created which is rich in opportunities for a particular type of growth to take place.

Environments of every type contain opportunities to unfold an orderly growth. In this case people are encouraged to straighten their backs, take a break from their toil in the fields and factories, and lift their eyes toward the sky. Cycles are created and fed. Mental and emotional stimulation is generated. Anything that excites the interest of a section of the community fulfills the common subconscious mind and its intricate steering processes. Prophecy finds a role in this area.

People in the physical must accost and feel into a sense of wonder, that which is unknowable. This exercises areas of the mind that must be exercised, but receive no stimulation from mundane work. Something is created within them that otherwise would not be created. The Organism changes slightly as a result.

Des: So the actual outcome of the prophecy is not important?

A: This is not so important, although prophecy is a process that can have a precise and literal outcome. More often there will be variables and interpretations. In the absence of clear evidence, the prophecy continues to be of value to the individual as well as the Organism.

Des: More so than if the prophecy were identified as being either completely true or completely false?

A: Yes.

Des: So people like Nostradamus devoted their life to creating a nothing, for whatever reason, lovingly nurturing a vacuum at the bidding of spirit?

A: Certainly not. His influence continues to permeate the common subconscious mind, a process driven by the individual in spirit who initiated the prophecy in the first place.
Des: He was and is acting on behalf of the Organism?
A: Yes.

March 16, 2008 The Antichrist and Demons
Des: I've been thinking of what you said about the value of the unknowable. Presumably theological conceptions like the Antichrist are necessary, because they are unknowable?
A: The value of encouraging people to engage in abstract and emotionally charged preoccupations must be acknowledged. In the case of prophecies and the Antichrist, it is a different type of stimulus.

With the Antichrist, clearly this concept comes in useful for a religious organization that falls back on the psychological fact that an enemy, real or invented, draws people together and makes them more easily influenced. This increases the strength of the organization. But this does not make the Church cynical and manipulative. Consider two facts.

On the one hand, congregations come together because they have common interests, common emotional needs to satisfy. The Church meets those needs. Where a need exists it will be met according to natural law. As people become more mature and sophisticated their focus moves and the organization moves with them. This could hardly be called cynical or manipulative.

On the other hand the Antichrist is real. He has been created out of the fabric of consciousness by those believing in him. But as growth takes place and people change their beliefs, the nature of the Antichrist changes. The being, the creation, actually changes because those who have created him go on to create something slightly different.

Des: Interesting! Do you have any comments about demons, infidels, and those in countries whose beliefs apparently consign them to hell?

A: We are clothing ideology, symbols and negative emotions with words that fit one culture or another. Those in physical continue to create negative realities and broadcast them within consciousness. The Antichrist, demons and all the rest of it defer to the laws of polarization holding sway in the physical. If there is a Christ there must be an Antichrist. If there is an angel there must be a demon. With both your infidels and Christian non-believers, blind historical alliances run through the landscape. They represent a rich vein of conflict to be mined for both individualization and spiritual growth.

Because emotions are polarized, the concepts and symbols they produce are polarized. Positive and negative realities are formed. With the latter, the opportunity is presented for people to agree, disagree, be tolerant and to redirect bad emotions. If there is nothing to forgive, the quality of forgiveness cannot be unfolded. If there is no opportunity to encounter disagreement, then compromise and cooperation cannot be developed.

March 19, 2008 Evolution versus Creationism

Des: Which is true, the scientific theory of evolution or the fundamentalist Christian theory of creationism?

A: Putting aside the fact that both are true because a significant section of the population emotionally has invested in one theory or the other, we would invite you to look at two possibilities. A liberal interpretation of both theories suggests that creationism, by whatever name, has produced the evolutionary process.

Des: A liberal interpretation would change the meaning of creationism and intelligent design. We'd be talking about something different, as with the theory of evolution and natural selection.

A: My comments hold. Because there is no such thing as time, we will have to forget the time factor. Yes, we know that both theories depend on it.

Des: You're playing with my head.

A: The second possibility is this. The competing theories fulfill the principle that physical life demands a measure of conflict, if only emotional conflict in this case. But then, there is no conflict that is not emotional conflict, and indeed there is no journey that is not an emotional journey.

March 20, 2008

Des: Because the book we are channeling answers a lot of questions, does this fact not undermine the principle that imponderables, unanswered questions and abiding mysteries are necessary to promote individuality and evolvement?

A: That will give you something to think about, Des.

Des: You do have a sense of humor.

A: And we've almost given you the last word.

March 22, 2008 Alien Life Forms
Des: We create collectively. Do we create extraterrestrials?
A: An extraterrestrial life form is an energy field which may impinge on the Organism. An individual in physical encountering such a life form will undergo a process in which his mind attempts to identify and interpret what he has encountered. His mind, quite beyond the level of conscious awareness, continues to reinterpret the energy field until it presents him with an object he can relate to, make sense of and recognize. His mind presents him with a signature of the energy field, a signature which he himself has created. In interpreting the energy field he has created an extraterrestrial.

As more extraterrestrials are encountered, this process changes. With every alien encounter, remember there is no time, a message is fed from the individual involved into the common subconscious mind in the usual way. A predisposition progressively becomes established within the common subconscious. Every interface with an extraterrestrial energy field subsequently comes to produce the same interpretation in the mind of the person encountering the energy field. A template, a mental/emotional pattern has been created.

While the individual has created the signature by drawing on the template, any resulting communication would be driven by the extraterrestrial energy field. An extraterrestrial is a valid being in its own right as is the human being.

Des: Can you tell me anything about the collective energy field of the extraterrestrials? To what sort of civilization do they belong?

A: Of course an alien civilization has its own history and aspirations, its own eternal journey, none of it in physical form.

Des: I guess such things could not be known for sure?

A: The further we become removed from our own backyard, the less we know. You are also becoming aware of pushing the limits of our common language.

Des: Is it possible to tell me how the extraterrestrial Organism relates to the energy field which you described as having created the Human Organism?

A: We are not able to answer your question, Des.

Des: Can communication with the extraterrestrial energy field take place in spirit?

A: To answer this we would have to develop new analogies with you.

Des: The accounts I've read about people encountering extraterrestrials, do these have any reality?

A: Beyond what we've told you, a new infrastructure of analogies would be required to introduce additional details.

March 24, 2008

Des: Why has the information you have been giving me, not been made known before, even in a more generalized version?

A: The information is provided when people can relate to it. A natural law is that nothing can be received from spirit until the physical community is ready. Common sense makes the same comment. At every point in history there have been ordinary people in one village or another who were able to communicate with spirit. Because they were representative of their community, they could receive only what the people in the community could understand.

Des: Otherwise they would pick up nothing, I guess.

A: They would receive a very generalized version that departed only slightly from what was already known.

Des: I seem to receive everything or nothing.

A: You get what serves the agenda of those who drive the conduit. The circumstances are quite different. You also have available the neuropsychological modality you call IADC®.

XVII. The Prophets Who Guide Us

March 25, 2008
Des: You said that never in the history of the human race has there been a person in physical who was more than a normal, fallible individual. Clearly this is intended to include religious figures. Could you comment?
A: It is this fact that makes human civilization so inspiring. There would be nothing inspiring if our achievements had been cobbled together by a superman or a Christ.
Des: How does this mesh with the natural law stating that every religion was created collectively by human mind out of consciousness? Why would we not produce a creation that inspires us with everything noble in terms of human achievement?
A: We would do that. The creation we talk about is the ordinary human being who achieves everything a Christ could achieve. We said that every situation and every individual is embraced and empowered by a unique web of natural laws. The web is qualified by a wealth of influences and counter-influences woven together, many of them unknowable. You can see how difficult it

was to create the analogies necessary to carry such complicated and qualified concepts, and then a language to carry them, but especially the means to make you familiar with the language, considering that no template existed within the common subconscious mind to facilitate this process.

Des: Thank you. Yes.

March 26, 2008 Why Does Illness Occur?

Des: Another question off our pile. Why does disease persist? New pathogens seem to emerge as soon as the old ones are defeated, as though they meet a compelling need.

A: Illness is produced out of consciousness because it is an agent of the process of evolvement. If an orderly unfoldment of potential did not need illness, then illness would not exist. At the physical level there is a need for disease and suffering as much as a need for food. As you change your ways through the process of growth, disease will disappear. We have touched on the natural law called Justice, the comfort accompanying good behavior and the discomfort accompanying bad behavior. Diseases are examples of these influences at play.

Des: On one or two occasions your answers have seemed slightly contrived, certainly lacking in qualifying details that would make them more complete. I suppose that's inevitable if you must resort to analogies.

A: Very much. The question of focus and priorities is important with analogous conceptions. The conduit accesses a lot more detail than has been available in the past. At this time it is quite adequate.

March 27, 2008 Euthanasia

Des: I'm supposed to ask about euthanasia.

A: Euthanasia is one of those mechanisms, along with abortion, which plays into the hands of individualization. It is not right or wrong. It provides raw material to be used by the individual to create an aspect of himself that otherwise would not be created. To that extent, the decision and the action flowing from it produce a slightly different personality.

Admittedly people involved in the decision do so at the spiritual level. An accord is reached. The action usually follows.

There can be complications. A difference of freewill opinion may develop between the logical, thinking mind of a family member helping with the decision and the person who is gravely ill. The family member may want to prolong the other's life, while the sick person may wish to die. Either party may experience a conflict between the logical, thinking mind and the spirit. It is possible that the interplay of negative and positive energy in physical overrides and skews the aspirations of spirit, the accord that has been reached. Such conflicts are raw material in the hands of individualization.

Des: One would imagine that this spirit mind versus physical mind thing explains a lot of the negative behavior encountered in physical, which would hardly be initiated in spirit.

A: This is very much the case. An immature spirit expressing itself within a physical body, can quite easily be submerged and swept away by negative energy. A more mature spirit personality is better equipped to assert itself and ensure that its agenda prevails. This principle holds across a range of physical experiences.

With euthanasia it pays to remember that the removal of one's physical body, especially at the end of a long life, is a small matter. Except for one consideration, namely that every second spent in the physical provides a uniquely valuable gift.

April 12, 2008 The Betrayal of Mother Teresa by God

Des: In Time magazine, *(September 3, 2007)* I read a comprehensive article about the late Mother Teresa, the Saint of the Gutters. In letters to her Church superiors she wrote that she had been given revelations from God as a young woman, but waited in vain throughout her long life for another word. It never came. Her trust and hope were greeted with silence. *(She wrote to the Rev. Michael van der Peet in September 1979, "Jesus has a very special love for you. [But] as for me, the silence and the emptiness is so great that I look and do not see, listen and do not hear.")*

The Church came up with various theological explanations in an effort to explain away what could be viewed as a betrayal by God. Mother Teresa apparently came to despair as she sought answers to her dark secret, *"Tell me, Father, why is there so much pain and darkness in my soul?" (August 1952.)* Doubtless she felt the burden of being an inspiration to millions who believed she had a special and close relationship with God. Can you help me to make sense of all this? What does she make of it after a decade in spirit?

A: We can say this, Mother Teresa is now aware that the reality she carried in physical was one that she wove for herself. If she felt betrayed by God, she created that betrayal because she alone put in place a lifetime's isolation from what she perceived as God's presence. As a young nun, her simple and intense trust included no such isolation and therefore she facilitated the communication.

Des: What changed?

A: As a young adult her almost childlike faith, her willingness to believe, her devout enthusiasm, temporarily elevated her above a dark emotional stream running through her psyche, which emerged from the springs of childhood. As the years passed this turbid presence gained prominence. Teresa, emotionally failing to acknowledge her childhood conflicts, became entrapped by them. The events of her adult life tended to awaken them, triggering the emotions she had lived during her upbringing.

Because the devout nun came to feel she was undeserving and inadequate, and because she was awash with the child's guilt, she immersed herself emotionally in a reality she felt she deserved. Her inner demons emerged. She wondered why almighty God would notice her, a scrawny kid whom nobody ever noticed. The emotional landscape across which Teresa trudged during the physical life she created for herself, was devoid of God's presence because she felt she was unworthy. At the same time she felt she was deceiving her followers, who looked up to her as God's ambassador in the physical. Her guilt was fed, thrusting her further into her childhood inadequacies. As so often is the case with people in physical, Teresa's childhood created the reality in which she spent most of her life.

Des: Why didn't she create what she most needed? I understand that Catholics believe that God visits his presence on those whose faith makes it appropriate.

A: We have just explained that, Des.

Des: What do you make of the theological positioning and repositioning of the Catholic hierarchy, as they sought to make understandable what they found in Teresa's journals after her death?

A: Theology is theology. It is what they do.

XVIII. Death Throes of Christianity?

April 2, 2008

Des: Statistics generally indicate that the Christian Church is like a dying tree. Although some branches remain greener than others, the outcome is inevitable. Can you comment?

A: We disagree with your attitude to this whole subject, Des. Some time ago you listened in on an admittedly good-natured discussion drawing a parallel between the behavior of Nazi Germany during the Second World War and the behavior of the established Church in Europe during The Middle Ages. But there is no parallel.

Church attitudes during The Middle Ages reflected the norms of the time. That is how people interacted. It was part of an orderly unfoldment of social conscience. The actions of Nazi Germany which entrapped a great number of decent German citizens represented an outrage, a stain on the collective conscience. It ran completely counter to the social standards of the Twentieth Century.

We have discussed Adolf Hitler's role in the affairs of Europe, and how his appearance gave expression to negative energy dominating European societies. The Church has been given a substance and reality by those believing in it. This belief structure developed in stages within the fabric of consciousness.

It follows that when the needs of people change, their beliefs change because beliefs mirror needs. The Church as it exists will change. It will adapt. Like those ever adaptive trees, eventually it will die. People will continue to create changing belief systems and give them reality. The new beliefs will give ground to changing needs, and different beliefs will be spawned, new religions, before they give way to others. Growth means change. Consciousness means growth.

Instead of looking at a dying tree in isolation, look at a forest. Trees die, even as saplings rise to replace them. There is nothing wrong or surprising about that. The Church grew to meet a collective need. When the existing Church ceases to thrive something else will grow to replace it.

Des: The same can be said of all religions, philosophies and belief structures.
A: Of course.

April 3, 2008 Can Past Lives Be Resolved in the Present?
Des: Talking about one of these belief structures, I was told from spirit that past life stuff influencing us in the present can be resolved by our present actions.
A: First to be considered is the fact that there is no time, once separation from the physical has been achieved. So there is no time between one physical life and

another, although obviously we are not talking about a continuation of lives as though they were one. A break is necessary to obtain a different genetic makeup for each physical journey, different upbringing experiences, a different timeframe, and the opportunity for one life to influence following ones, especially the one immediately following. Patterns of cause and effect link the different lives, the fact notwithstanding that they all take place at the same instant of time.

Des: It's hard to imagine the process of cause and effect taking place in an environment where there is no time.

A: Because you have no concepts we can use to make an explanation understandable, no explanation is possible. The process of cause and effect linking different lives is a natural law promoting growth and individualization. Free will is used to act on the sometimes powerful influences extending from past lives. The weaknesses of the past life, presented to an individual in the present, gives that person the chance to work on them, but with the benefit of a different physical vehicle and different aptitudes. Because there is no time, it can be said that present actions and insights can be injected into the past life. Therefore past-life stuff can be resolved in the present life.

Des: I'm aware of the limitations of an analogy, but even so it seems to me that some explanations are rather thin porridge as far as depth and detail goes. Am I being unfair?

A: You are not being unfair to seek an answer you can understand. Every explanation must begin with the most basic facts, and build from there. These pages represent the most basic facts. In time we will build on them.

April 7, 2008 The Spirit Hierarchy

Des: When I look at human behavior in the physical, it occurs to me that not very much is perfect. This must reflect on those steering the Organism. I understand that the process of trial and error extends to the top of the Christmas tree. Accountability! Is there something I am missing?

A: There are no mistakes as such. Trial and error is a learning mechanism. Nothing has gone wrong. The process in which free will creates the individual person and every person added together, all the way to the top, is the perfection of nature.

Having said that, an interesting point is raised. Every person who is privileged to represent the Organism learns by the same process familiar to everyone. Trial and error is involved. We all have free will. We are all fallible. We belong to one family, and at a meaningful level we love and rely on one another. The types of lessons which are available change the further up the tree one climbs. People learn different lessons as they face different challenges.

Des: What types of things?

A: We look at the direction in which the human community should seek to move, what direction is most likely to serve the aspirations of the species. Which options are to be encouraged and which discouraged, always bearing in mind that emotional input into the common subconscious mind is a powerful part of the process. Also significant is the fact that every individual human being is embraced by a unique web of natural law, and so responds to the common subconscious mind differently.

Des: Which is important in the case of world leaders, I guess.

A: Exactly. We possess the enablement to set in motion cycles which can steer outcomes, and influence delicate balances. But we are always fenced within the boundaries of natural law, which demands that free will must have the final say. Free will in physical defines and shapes the total Human Organism.

Des: I see. So in physical we are guided by spirit. Then who guides your deliberations?

A: You do! We are guided from the physical and from every level of spirit. The Human Organism is just that, a single body of awareness, one part relying on another just as one part of your physical body relies on every other part.

Des: You exercise an executive function of some sort, in some measure.

A: Depending on which analogy we select in order to discuss the question.

Des: Why does this feel like it's going nowhere fast?

A: We can answer the query. The Organism is a gestalt. It is made up of more than the total of its individual parts. Exactly what the additional factor is remains unknown and probably unknowable.

Des: Does it exercise any influence on the physical?

A: Of course, because it's an integral part of the Organism. The presence of this unknown factor is hardly surprising when you consider that the Organism itself has been constructed within the consciousness of a greater body, which gave it form and a separate identity.

Des: Where does the so-called Entity come into this?

A: The Entity is quite different. It is nothing more than a hypothetical concept that enables us to identify what cannot be identified. It goes like this. Something is there. This fact is unquestionable. It is removed from what we refer to as consciousness. It is a source of intelligence. We are not aware of having contact with it or being influenced by it.

Des: I understand you possess the information you have about it because your sphere of responsibility gives you the entitlement.

A: That is right. Various areas of awareness become part of me. That is what I am. You have asked about other information I have. Every person embraces a unique web of natural law. Mine includes that degree of enablement, as is the case with other beings of similar maturity. My awareness is stepped through that part of the Organism located in spirit, and made available to every single individual according to his ability to relate to and accept it. That becomes part of the person's web of natural law.

Des: But this is not the case in the physical.

A: One of the limitations of the physical is the need for emotional isolation, one person from another. I extend an influence into the physical via the common subconscious, which enables isolation to be maintained.

XIX. Heaven and Hell

April 14, 2008

Des: Christianity seems to be preoccupied on occasion with the subject of heaven and hell. Presumably it's all just a state of mind, a metaphor, a symbol?

A: Everything is a state of mind, a simplification tailored so people can make sense of what is being said, a doorway into a greater reality. The many religions are nothing more than beliefs that were created by people seeking to meet their needs. That doesn't make different religions wrong or less necessary or even less real in the unfoldment of human potential.

On the subject of heaven and hell, you are in hell now in the physical. You are in the only place in the human universe where limitation, suffering and conflict may be encountered of such extreme intensity. That is what the physical is, a few heartbeats that are insufferable, but which build a foundation, individual and collective, lasting forever and making everything possible. The physical plane is the beating heart of the natural law called individualization.

Des: And when one dies?

A: Remember what happened when your wife died. Nothing changed. There was no break in her consciousness. She noticed no difference. For a time she dwelt within the same fear, abject misery and aloneness she suffered as her body died around her. It could be said that her continuing trauma shortly after death also was hell, but that merely was an extension of the same experience. The word "hell" has no meaning beyond that given to it by one belief structure or another. Heaven could be likened to the state in which she now finds herself, a serenity, a sense of completeness, a creative excitement, a fullness of love for which no physical word exists. But this situation is inescapable and denied to nobody regardless of their physical circumstances.

Des: Denied to nobody?

A: That is right. The rewards associated with heaven, elitism and social manipulation, owe everything to the particular beliefs that have been collectively created, nurtured and changed over a period of time.

Des: And not by natural law?

A: Well, natural law put in place the means through which this process functions.

April 18, 2008 The God-Man Dying on the Cross

Des: Yet another belief system has it that a God-man called Jesus died on the cross so that mankind could be cleansed of its sins. This is a recurring theme in several religions throughout the ages *(Osiris, Prometheus, Horus, Jesus)*. Exactly what is so significant and enduring in this concept?

A: Even if we choose the representative example of Jesus, a simple premise is recognizable. A sacrifice or selfless act is made in the name of love, representing what is most noble in human behavior. Another person or other people benefit. A human being has spoken in a language that is universal. An example is provided for the guidance of others. A cycle is set in motion. A shift, big or small, takes place in the polarized balance between positive energy and the vast sea of negative energy.

Let us look at some examples.

A mother alone with her children and without adequate support, sacrifices any luxuries and a social life for years to meet their needs. Not only her children but their children in turn are likely to benefit from this mother's devotion.

A soldier acts on his decision to jeopardize or sacrifice his life in order to save a number of his comrades.

A caregiver puts aside the rewards of a family of her own in order to look after a chronically disabled parent.

A breadwinner immerses himself for two or three decades in seventy-hour work weeks so that he can support and educate a large family.

Des: Do you think this total self-sacrifice is healthy? I was told that we are here to attend to our own growth, but in a balanced way.

A: A balance certainly is necessary. Your guidance was talking about the person who needlessly makes sacrifices for others in a self-pitying manner, or who does so because he has other self-indulgent or self punishing motives. Another person may act in the same way, because mindlessly and automatically he is copying a parent's behavior, due to childhood programming. Yes, self sacrifice can be unhealthy. This is not what we started to talk about.

Des: Okay.

A: To return to self-sacrifice as a noble gesture, the picture of Jesus suffering on the cross represents a symbol that speaks eloquently to a positive face of human nature.

Des: For some reason the idea of an explanation being gift wrapped in a pretty box called an analogy is unsatisfying to me. It lacks substance and depth. Perhaps that's the engineer inside my mind. I know it's my problem.

A: It is nobody's problem. You enable explanations to be made. Imagine what it would be like if you attempted to explain in great detail to a class of pre-school children what television was all about. You might concentrate first on the electronics engineering aspects of transmission and reception. Then you might move to the implications of different types of programs on socio-economic groupings within the community. Finally you might focus on the psychology of violent TV content as it affects adults, adolescents and children in different countries.

You would have to resort to drawing simple word pictures to which the children could relate. To achieve that you would forge a common language, which would need to be familiar to them, yet adequate to accommodate the simplest concepts. Invariably when your explanations to the little ones were analyzed later on, they would be lacking in substance and depth. Your

comments about Jesus on the cross and about self-sacrifice are understandable.
Des: Thank you. A final thought for the day, to move even further away from the focus, what would you say to Hitler or Pol Pot or Stalin if you were to encounter them?
A: The same you would say to those pre-school children.

XX. The Second Coming of Jesus Christ

April 22, 2008

Des: Presumably the Second Coming of Jesus Christ must take place for those who believe in it. I understand it is a cornerstone of the Christian faith. When will it happen? How will people be involved who do not believe in the Second Coming, and who have not participated in the creation of the event?

A: As far as non-believers or those of other faiths are concerned, one doesn't have to believe in an event to be overtaken by it. A spell of beautiful unseasonable weather, even if you have not given the matter any thought, still affects you.

Sections of the human community create out of consciousness what they believe. Different sections believe different things, produce different creations. Natural law provides for this. The creations interact at the physical level in an orderly and inescapable way, in terms of how the events are interpreted and in objective terms. Natural law is a framework around which the Organism and its physical expression are constructed. It is not meaningful to suggest that natural law somehow visits itself on the Human Organism to make it work. The beliefs of Christianity will influence those in physical who have no interest in the Christian faith. The most important point is even conservative Christians, influenced by the modern world, are coming to an awareness that the foretold Second Coming may be a symbolic event rather than a physical one. There are different ways in which a heaven on earth can be ushered in! People create within consciousness along these lines. The constantly changing shape of Christianity enables those in its different streams and denominations to draw from the broad belief structure that which fits more comfortably with modern attitudes.

Des: So every individual Christian drinks from this philosophical creation and changes it in the process.

A: Mainly it nurtures emotionally. Every single human being is treated differently from every other, having a web of natural law according to the demands of unfoldment. Every person communes with her own God.

Des: There are as many gods as there are people. There are as many realities as there are people.

A: That is right.

Des: So for every question there are billions of answers.

A: I think we understand the limitations of an analogy, Des. The point can now be made that the Second Coming will never arrive as a direct physical event.

Des: A lot of Christians will be challenged!

A: And a lot will not, because their expectations will bear fruit. A great many Christians can embrace the symbol of a heaven on Earth, and may go on to give it expression using their faith to bring it about. They can feed the hungry, cease being judgmental, stop discrimination, support all in need and nurture societies that would benefit. They can help drain anger and hatred from communities, and the cycles being created. At that point many of the diseases afflicting the physical will disappear. Suffering and disease will not be necessary. The so-called defense industry will wither, freeing up funding for more worthy causes.

There is no reason why these changes cannot take place at the physical level, but not because Jesus appears in the sky accompanied by a host of angels. Natural law can be served in a different way. It is possible that the promised Second Coming, the appearance of perfect love in the physical, will make an appearance as expected, if not in the manner that was expected.

Des: Indirectly.

A: Perhaps this could never come to pass were it not for the example of Jesus on the cross. That symbol may have the power to stir the awareness of the Christian community, and produce outcomes which otherwise would not be produced. If this were to happen, futures would open to the human condition that otherwise could not exist. Jesus and the entire Christian infrastructure were created out of consciousness. Free will was involved, created and continues to adapt this living process. The future continues to be steered by ordinary human beings.

Des: In the absence of time, presumably Christian attitudes in our future will feed back and affect the nature of the Christian religion in the present?

A: Even now you are toying with the question of which future is going to emerge from unfolding events. Such consideration is not a part of our agenda.

XXI. The Book's Dedication

April 25, 2008

Des: To whom or what do you want your book dedicated?

A: We can leave that to your free will. You are a unique, eternal unit of consciousness focused on and unfolding itself. You are alone, and in different ways always will be. The people and objects in your environment are just items removed from what you are and present only to stimulate awareness of yourself. At the end of the day there will only be you in the universe, because you will be that universe. At that time you will have taken to yourself every thought, emotion and physical experience of every second. You will have embraced and incorporated everyone and everything you have ever loved. You will be every negative lesson you have ever encountered, but only its positive outpouring. You will know perfect balance and perfect contentment. And that is only the beginning. The same can be said of every human being.

Des: So it is, this book is dedicated to me, because that's all there is.

XXII Questions and Answers

Philosophical Questions
Q: Information from "A" seems to be different from Val's, but is supposed to come from the same place.
Des: As the book progresses, more and more details are incorporated into any given subject, which may give the appearance of a difference of opinion. Although direct involvement from "A" made additional information available, I am not aware of any fundamental difference between his explanations and Val's.
Q: Are there people in spirit, even Beings of Light, who have never been in physical form?
Des: This subject was not included in the agenda to be propagated.
Q: Beings of Light fascinate me. I prefer to call them angels. Will someone like Mother Teresa, or the Pope, or an historical or political figure who helps thousands of people, become an angel?
Des: This is one subject I discussed with spirit but have not

included in The Littlest Crusade. The answer is probably. An important point is what motivated the historical or political figure to be so generous. Perhaps a craving for popularity and more power, an effort to impress superiors, or some other self-serving reason. If so, that person would be very modest and certainly not a Being of Light.

Mother Teresa influenced millions of people, either through her organizations or as an inspiration. She is a beautiful and spiritual Being of Light who shone a healthy radiance into her various environments while in physical.

An equally giving and loving person who influenced only a single individual, say her invalid mother, at the expense of her own comfort and satisfactions, may enjoy a spiritual status no less than Mother Teresa. Yes, Mother Teresa's world teemed with millions of people while Unknown Teresa's world was dominated by one other person. No matter how many people occupy it, an environment is an environment, comprising what is beyond the person, what is outside her own being. This applies to everyone.

How an individual responds to the person or people in her surroundings creates that individual at the spiritual level, second by second and decade by decade. That creation is what she takes back to spirit when she dies. That is what she becomes, whether she was an atheist or the Saint of the Gutters.

Q: As a thinking man I believe that no evidence exists pointing to life after death. Anecdotal accounts can be explained quite adequately in rational, scientifically validated terms. What do you think of that?

Des: I think you should stand by your beliefs. I respect them as I respect you for making them known. Perhaps people should weigh your viewpoint but be guided by their own conclusions.

Q: You seem to be saying, nothing is real. Nothing we do is wrong. The world is whatever we think it should be. Don't you feel a bit like a dry leaf floating in the breeze? Where is your sense of control and direction in life?

Des: Forget for the moment that the message is not mine. I believe we should not hurt ourselves or others, either by actions or omissions. Beyond that nothing we do is wrong. That stance calls for self-respect and respect for others. It also demands a high level of personal and social responsibility and accountability.

Perhaps a person should not judge another but rather seek to understand his behavior. Many negative cycles are driven by discrimination, disadvantage or lack of support, and the coping strategies produced. The foregoing attitudes reflect my personal sense of control and direction in life.

Q: Nothing is real?

Des: Let's ask ourselves what reality actually is. Four-year-old Johnny is distraught because the kids at pre-school draw attention to his big ears and call him Dumbo. Even if he does have unusually large ears, Mother would persuade him that his ears are quite normal, "There's nothing wrong with your ears or any other part of you. In fact, you are perfect. Promise me, Johnny, that you will never change because I love you exactly as you are."

Mother is dismissing an undeniable reality and creating a more significant reality, the need to promote her son's positive self-esteem and self-confidence. Mother is accepting responsibility for building shells of reality, a greater reality overlaying and superseding a smaller one. She is acting as I would act. In that context, perhaps we should ask ourselves if there is such a thing as an absolute reality.

The world is whatever we think it should be. Although I wouldn't put it like that, I do try to unfold a personal world within me that is as noble as I can.

Q: How?

Des: I think of a perfect environment. Then I try to create it in the tiny microcosm of which I am the center. I follow my advice to others, "Be the world you would like to see." I fail sometimes, but my best has to do. All these sentiments can be recognized in the pages of the book.

Q: What exactly is the conscience?

Des: It is the involvement of the spirit mind within the physical mind. It could be called a steering mechanism providing guidance as the person navigates between positive and negative energy. Nevertheless, free will has the final say, because the person remains free to do what he chooses, even though he knows which action is right and which is wrong.

Q: Will science on this planet ever become aware of the truth, the whole truth and nothing but the truth, so help me natural law?

Des: I understand that never will humanity be aware of ultimate truths, ultimate realities. This is the nature of the human condition. This is what we are. In a thousand years, those in the forefront of scientific enquiry may possess a billion times more factual information. But what there is to know may have increased by infinity.

Q: How and why?

Des: Consciousness, the sum total of all life and what it produces, expands with every thought, emotion and action of every life form in every universe. If the understanding of the Human Organism were able to keep up, the species would not be human but something else, something far superior in terms of development. At least this is the information available through the conduit.

Q: If we are talking about humanity following the genetic mutations which were discussed, would this reasoning still hold? Given that situation, invariably humanity will be something far superior than it is now in terms of development.

Des: I don't know. Such details fall outside the agenda of the conduit. The people originating the information seem intent on making known a few important facts that could modify behavior at the physical level in the immediate future. Having said this, I know what their answer would be. The extent of the mutation, and its particular characteristics, will be dictated by your collective activities in the short term.

Q: The people you channel sometimes sound as though they are bent on changing the world order. Do they think that changing the attitude of a few human beings can alter the way things are done on the planet?

Des: Yes, a few at a time. Nothing else has worked in the past. Anyway there is no such thing as failure. It's just that some avenues into the future are less bumpy than others. Growth is growth. Growth is inescapable. We grow despite ourselves.

Q: Animals killing one another to survive. That seems a twisted comment on the perfection of Mother Nature.

Des: An animal is able to switch off its consciousness, separate its awareness from the flesh, so there is neither stress nor discomfort. The victim is abruptly in another place. Once the animal's fate is sealed, trauma would serve no useful purpose. The same applies to people in the normal course of events, once survival seems to be impossible.

Q: You have talked about the limitations of physical life. I'm not sure I understand exactly what you mean.

Des: Anything in physical that limits one being comfortable and relaxed, fulfilled, happy, safe, and complete as a human being. The inescapable results of the aging process, the conflicts of childhood and adolescence when dysfunction exists within the family, destructive social and political cycles, poverty, illness including physical, mental and emotional illness, and relationship stresses in the home and the outside world. We are talking about the ever-present and toxic effects of negative energy on every aspect of life.

Q: "A" is upfront about what we are not doing right. But he is less upfront in providing specific guidance. What's wrong with some advice on the hows and whys?

Des: Their agenda is focused on providing an oversight so we can examine alternatives. Also provided is a general scenario that can be expected to unfold if our activities remain unaltered. Behavior is not likely to change unless some incentive is present, and this book goes a tiny distance into providing an incentive. At that point the responsibility becomes ours. Whether or not our communities become more caring, or are willing to be guided, is up to us.

We will never be told how to go about it, because we are in physical to make these decisions and create ourselves in the process individually and collectively. We are what we create. This cannot be done for us.

Q: I still can't work out how free will rules the universe, when there is no time as such. At one level or another, why not go forward, have a look at outcomes and then go back and make the necessary arrangements? This would make nonsense of free will.

Des: The point is made that both the concepts of time and free will are expressed as analogies. One fact out of every thousand is presented. These facts are put together as a word picture to make a simple explanation possible. Because we could not understand a more complex explanation, the means do not exist to make one available. The agenda which was pushed through the conduit was shaped according to our needs at this time.

Free will is an absolute reality. So is the absence of time. How you relate to these two facts, and make use of them, is made understandable with the help of these simple analogies. Of course any analogy is limited in the number of explanations it can provide and the depth of understanding it can make possible.

Your question interests me for another reason, however. "A" has taken you forward in time so you can have a look at outcomes! Now that you have come back, it's up to you to make the necessary arrangements, the changes to your lifestyle that have been suggested.

Q: What do I say to the Pope when he talks of the absolute reality of evil and makes known his views on the one-and-only unalterable truth according to the Bible?

Des: That would depend on the interpretation you choose to place on his words, which is a matter for you alone. You are involved in the process of creating yourself uniquely, in small part according to what you make of this particular Christian perspective. The Pope's comments are less important than what you decide to do about them. The responsibility is yours. He is merely an influence in your environment to enable you to create. What you create becomes yours alone.

Q: How does Hitler's mother feel at the moment about her son Adolf? Does she accept some responsibility?

Des: She feels as everyone does after surviving the blowtorch of physical life. She takes from the situation what her level of growth permits her to take. She reaches out for learning and wraps herself in its folds. She is supported, encouraged, accepted and uplifted by those in her greater group but especially those in her inner group. Love is love.

Q: Wars, pestilence and so on are made appropriate because natural law says we must suffer if we are to learn to be better human beings. I can accept that. Why did the influenza epidemic following World War One have to take place that killed another fifty to one hundred million people? There are plenty of other examples where serial episodes of suffering took place that apparently had no link to a need for widespread changes in behavior.

Des: The same principle holds for every case, even if different types of behavior modification are involved.

Following World War One the necessary lessons had not been learned. A further push was required. Significantly, the influenza pandemic in many cases affected a different section of the international community than the war did. Even the two together were not sufficient. History tells us that the aftermath of World War One made almost inevitable the onset of World War Two within the same generation.

Q: Is it possible for a very spiritually mature or evolved individual to avoid negative energy while in physical?

Des: Only in degree. During sleep the person can be immersed in unconscious activities, bad dreams and persisting negative emotions, according to the agenda the person came to physical to resolve. I have heard the term *night terrors* used to describe the phenomenon. This unconscious activity often relates to events in the past, especially in childhood, when the person was an innocent victim.

Nobody can completely avoid the effects of bereavement, health problems, crime, discrimination or accidents. This is what they came to physical searching out, this is why they are here. A spiritually mature personality is likely to respond to suffering in a more philosophical and accepting way, being less self-centered and feeling the anguish less acutely.

After-Death Environment

Q: The people in spirit talk about different groups, almost as though they are referring to villages scattered around the landscape. Obviously this is not the case.

Des: No. Group members are drawn together by natural law because of emotional links. Each group is a single emotional organism. Its bonds continue to strengthen and evolve.

As a departure from this concept, a situation exists where the inner group or family, forms and dissolves and reforms depending on who is present. Tanya's family group comprises Val's family plus my family. If Tanya died as an adult, her friends and other people also would be included in her inner group. Individuals belonging to completely remote groups probably would be included, bound to her by positive emotional bonds. Likewise she would belong to their inner groups. But always at the center of each inner group is to be found the parents and their immediate and extended families.

As different individuals come and go the inner group tends to dissolve and reform as the emotional focus shifts to reflect the changing bonds and affinities. This process is comfortable, fluid, inescapable, and often involves members of the greater group. People from beyond the greater group who share no bond will not register on a spirit's awareness, but will register with another spirit with whom there is a bond. To that extent every personality in spirit has a unique inner group. With Tanya, who died before she was born, these links are much simpler.

At one juncture I asked whether Tanya's group affiliations, the people who register on her awareness, include those she has encountered in physical while sharing a group member's journey during the process of communication. The answer was that this matter fell outside the agenda of the conduit.

Q: I am adopted. Do I come from the same greater group in spirit, or even the same family group, as my birth parents? What about my adoptive parents?

Des: This varies. But does it matter? Electing to undergo a genetic or birth experience with one set of parents, and a nurturing upbringing with another, represents a decision that always is planned with infinite care, by every spirit with an involvement. There is always a sense of love and community. The possessiveness of physical life, its jealousies, rivalries and resentments are not present.

Q: Am I correct to assume that in physical we learn the lessons of life, but in spirit we merely re-examine them and extract the different perspectives they contain?

Des: In a narrow context the answer probably is yes. Nevertheless in extracting different perspectives from a physical lesson, the spirit personality is still learning. Very often the spirit is able to internalize areas of knowledge that had not been recognizable while in flesh. The spirit becomes further removed from heavy matter, and continues to pursue in greater depth different insights and oversights coming from the same activity in physical. And so every part of the journey informs again and again and again.

Yes, it is a reality that in physical the learning process is rapid and sometimes instantaneous, often forced, occasionally brutal. Conversely many lessons are available in spirit that could not possibly be understood in physical, because a more benign mental/emotional environment exists which enables more benign perspectives to be drawn from every situation.

Q: What changes take place once the spirit has escaped from the grip of physical life? I'm interested in detailed emotional stuff.

Des: Let's restrict this answer to the time shortly after death.

(1) A whole universe of insights unfolds once one's harsh judgments are put aside, the individual ceases to condemn and punish himself emotionally, once he no longer feels the need to compensate for real or imagined inadequacies. All this has been programmed into his mind from his physical journey.

(2) As soon as the fight to survive on a competitive physical landscape ceases to be necessary, the dog-eat-dog appetites start to ebb away. The individual relaxes. He becomes receptive to greater truths, and looks out over broader horizons.

(3) Soon he is able to acknowledge a more complete experience of love. He immerses himself in it, surrenders to its completeness.

(4) Once the illuminating presence of evolved personalities can be discerned he is awed and inspired by their beauty and power. He is transformed.

(5) A fierce need then prevails to give himself over to spiritual unfoldment and service to others. Flowing on, the self-creative process progressively claims his focus, along with its fierce and exhilarating commitment.

This emotional growth makes a parade of different perspectives available and inevitable as the individual continues to move away from heavy matter.

Val's Circumstances

Q: Your account of your wife's awful dilemma after she died frightened and discouraged me. Most readers want to be reassured. That's why they read.

Des: Val's circumstances before she died were as bad as any. For three years all she had to look forward to was choking to death or being hooked up to tubes as her body deteriorated around her. She was terrified without being able to communicate. Her post-death experiences were so severe, because her emotional pre-death experiences were. Such distress clearly is not typical.

This level of trauma notwithstanding, she admitted after attaining some distance from the physical that immediately after dying there was an awareness of relief and peace. No longer could anything bad happen to her. She became progressively more reconciled, relaxed and safe as she approached the proximity of family members who awaited her arrival.

Val's account during the weeks after her passing was colored by a sense of victimization and resentment directed to me. Only later her comments became more objective and balanced.

Q: After some time in spirit, Val said she saw your activities in a different light and forgave you for abandoning her in Emmerson House. Was that because the relative absence of negative energy prompted her to forgive, regardless of your behavior? *(This question came from one of Val's loyal lady friends.)*

Des: I applaud the fact you are acting on convictions you hold sincerely, in criticizing me. It makes you free. In the same manner my decisions about Val make me free.

Yes, I think the lack of negative energy comes into it. Also relevant is the fact that she eventually reached the point in spirit where she was able to re-examine the Emmerson era and understand my involvement, resources, spread of responsibilities and priorities. Once she disengaged from the suffering she saw a different reality.

Q: With your knowledge of life after death and the ultimate power of free will, why didn't you relieve your wife of so much suffering? Why didn't you facilitate her death?

Des: Because I don't break the law. That also is a free will decision. An important consideration is that at the spiritual level, Val put herself in Emmerson with careful calculation. It was part of her personal odyssey, including her responsibility to the conduit and the Organism. I knew this.

Q: Why does your wife, Val, know nothing about the so-called life review, which is a well-known phenomenon encountered when a person has a near-death experience and reviews the major events of his life before being resuscitated? Even if she did not personally experience one, surely her communication with other deceased personalities would have enabled her to learn indirectly through their experiences. Or "A" could have given her the details.

Des: Val and everyone else in that environment create and nurture their own unique unfoldment. A part of this process enables an individual to hone a particular aspect of his or her makeup, and step around another. In doing this Val omitted anything to do with the life review.

Mediumship, Psychism

Q: I sat in on a session with Val in which O'Shira was channeled. I am acquainted with the process and have had questions answered through a number of such channels. Although O'Shira's response could not possibly have come from Val herself, or been influenced by her, I found his attitude to be more authoritarian than I found comfortable, and his general philosophical outlook rigid and dogmatic compared with other channels. This surprised me. Can you help me to understand? The different channels all seem to provide a slightly different spin on any subject. But apparently it all comes from the same source.

Des: The section of this book on different writers channeling information, applies no less to Val and other trance channelers. In the case of O'Shira, who was not the only personality she channeled, I had the opportunity to note his delivery as well as his belief structure over many years, and observed the manner in which they seemed to change. I was able to question him during one-to-one sessions with Val.

An interesting fact emerged. Details coming from O'Shira were shaped and presented according to the ability of most of the people present to relate to and understand them. With different congregations different levels of sophistication were seen. As O'Shira's gatherings became more informed he showed them a different face. His guidance became more liberal, less authoritarian, rigid and dogmatic. As people felt able to accept responsibility for their own judgments he fashioned his teaching accordingly. He met their changing needs.

Q: What have your experiences been with your own guidance at different times of your life? Has your wife been involved? How has this affected you?

Des: Throughout much of my adult life I have been guided and instructed by spirit as some other people have, usually, but not always, at my instigation. I have no idea what they will say, even when I have asked the question. The answer can be quite removed from my personal opinions or belief structure, but never to the extent that I am unable to comprehend.

With the passage of time, as I was able to understand deeper and more complex issues, their information became more comprehensive. As a young child my clairaudient input was spontaneous and seemed to involve chatter that did not include me or acknowledge me. As a young adult the communication shifted focus to center around me, but in pragmatic rather than philosophical terms. I became involved in social interfaces with the people who were instructing me, discussions about our relationship during past lives together. I have almost no recollection of these conversations, doubtless a comment on their ability to block my mind as well as instruct it.

Val engaged in a similar psychic process. We were able to compare notes. Both sources spoke of our activities together in the future. I was intrigued that closely similar information came to us quite independently, and we discussed the matter from time to time over a period of years.

As multiple sclerosis tightened its grip on her mind and body, our relationship was destroyed in stages. Nevertheless she persisted with her trance channeling, always supported by a group of devoted friends. Then she attempted to self-medicate with drugs obtained over the internet. This led to a series of strokes that destroyed her body and left her as a tetraplegic, able to move nothing but her eyes and barely able to speak.

Some time later my guidance informed me that Val and I needed that experience to prepare us for our project together. I was not encouraged to obtain further details and have not pursued the matter. Since there is no such thing as an accident or a coincidence, it seems inescapable that every one of these events happened according to a painstakingly balanced plan, qualified only by the exercise of free will.

Q: If spirits supposedly are so happy and devoid of negative energy, how come they are sometimes seen to be in distress when communicating with people via a medium?

Des: I have never encountered this. Unless you are talking about those who never have progressed beyond the earthbound state, and so continue to dwell within the proximity of the material plane. These individuals are neither in one place nor another, and carry the same negative energy they carried in physical. They are not considered to be in spirit.

Q: Me thinks you have a vivid imagination and an appetite for hard work. May I suggest you made the whole thing up?

Des: You may. I think everyone who is interested should examine the evidence relating to all areas of life even viewpoints that conflict with your own. Be skeptical. Personally I have trouble accepting the premise of conservative Christianity that faith is sufficient, that we can settle for a trusting acceptance of what we are told in the Bible. No! Be hard-eyed, pragmatic and reluctant in all your philosophical evaluations, including this book.

Q: I'd really like to know more about aliens, alien energies. Could you obtain more information if you asked again?

Des: Sorry. I've tried. I'd like to know more as well. I'm just the postman.

Q: Is there anything you regret so far as your involvement with the conduit is concerned?

Des: I import emotions from spirit as well as philosophical information, and I have become aware of the privilege involved. The answer is no.

Q: Where do you stand in terms of spiritual maturity?

Des: I have no idea. Actually I'm not interested. I have a job to do and that is my only concern. I have never asked and never been told.

Q: Has there ever been a conflict between what you believe personally and what you have been fed from spirit?

Des: Many years ago there was. However as I received more detail from my guidance and was invited to question anything and everything, it was difficult not to defer to logic. Eventually their attitudes, aspirations and belief structures became mine. Sometimes it is difficult to determine where I start and where I finish. I suspect a lot of people are like that, especially creative people.

Once "A" started to drive the conduit, either through

Val or directly, I encountered less comfortable concepts again.

Q: Will other people be able to use IADC® and build on the details you have introduced via the conduit?

Des: That would depend on when and which future among many unfolds. I do know that from this point such an undertaking would be very much simpler, because the groundwork already has been done. A comprehensive framework has been put in place by this book. A template exists within the common subconscious mind which contains analogies along with their language of concepts. Previously none of this existed.

Q: You said you were prompted to ask questions. Why would you be prompted to ask questions for which answers were not available?

Des: If one question or another could not be answered, the opportunity presented itself for an explanation to be provided as to why. The conduit serves a particular agenda, and your question falls outside the agenda, or you are getting away from the focus of the original question. Every response was directed to the reader rather than to me, and the question I was prompted to ask was structured with that in mind.

Not every question was prompted. I was free to ask whatever I wanted. Once an initial question had received an answer, I needed to make sure I understood what was given to me.

Q: Evolution versus creationism. This is an interesting subject, but "A" chose to make a joke of it. Why?

Des: 1. He did answer the question by stating that the evolutionary process was created. He also inferred that neither theory should be taken literally.

2. I knew what he was saying, and could have asked for further clarification. It is my responsibility to make the details presented to me understandable to readers. I am doing so now with this explanation. There is no such thing as an accident or a coincidence, in terms of this question, its answer or in any other way.

3. His answer shows something of the good-natured attitude extended to me. This is a comment on "A" himself, the fact notwithstanding that he was positioned in a heavy, relatively negative, vibrational environment in order to communicate with me.

4. Further details about the evolution-creationism mystery are not included in the agenda that is part of the conduit.

Q: Much ado is made of individual and collective free will in the overall creative process. But the questions in this book that you asked of spirit were given to you to ask. There seems to be a conflict in terms of your personal free will. Many areas of your life seem to have been driven by spirit.

Des: In 1981 I agreed to take part with Val in a joint project the details of which were not provided. My free will came into that.

The circumstances that dominated my childhood, and equipped me to function within the conduit, were put in place by me, because prior to my birth I chose my parents and my various environments. I steered the journey, in large measure through the years that led eventually to my role in this book. My free will came into that.

At any time throughout my life I was able to change my mind or go off on a tangent. Nobody would have stopped me from opting out of my commitments to the project. I never did so. My free will came into that.

I was helped and guided throughout my life in various ways. I agreed to this, at one level or another, and allowed it to happen. My free will came into that.

But to answer on your query, yes, I was prompted to ask certain questions of spirit, but this was merely one part of my role in the conduit. I agreed to all aspects of my role. My free will came into that.

Religion

Q: You speak down to God. Who do you think you are?

Des: A god in training, perhaps? We all defer to a personal god whom we acknowledge so he or she or it can help meet our unique needs, and help unfold our resources. Some people might refer to this as a personal understanding of scripture or an interpretation of God's word. Others might worship a secular god. So be it.

In my case I tend to be pretty picky with my god. Some gods are better than others. A good god does not control or intimidate. With my god I won't have it! He must not command a god-fearing congregation. Instead he helps to support and enable one's potential like a wise parent, he inspires with love, nurtures with respect, heals and guides.

Zen Buddhism claims that we cannot learn the truth from sacred books. We need to look no further than ourselves, for this is where it is to be found, in every one of us. A personal god enables this to be done.

Q: What explains the almost instant change some Born-Again Christians talk about? They think their joyful experience proves the existence of a one and only God. Something must happen!

Des: They feel joy, a sense of release that results from their becoming whole. The Born-Again Christian is completing oneself with something beyond oneself, rising above the iron embrace of material life. The positive feelings represent a reward, according to natural law, for doing what is appropriate. She is creating the awareness within herself that she is in physical form in order to learn from it and rise above it. Love, humility, respect and a sense of shared interests and community with other Born-Again Christians also move her toward this goal. Other religions and denominations offer the same opportunity and the same reward. Material form is harsh in order to prompt the individual to uniquely rise above it.

Q: Why do you go on about things like the need for negative energy in the physical? It is not needed. All you have to do is deny Satan a place in your life by turning your back on him and embracing Jesus. You would do well to turn on the light, instead of studying the shadows on the curtain.

Des: Negative energy and polarization play a role in individualization, making every human being unlike every other.

Tanya

Q: Say a baby dies before being born. Those spirits, like Tanya, seem to encounter a pretty meager learning environment compared with a person spending ninety years in physical. Pretty thin porridge I would think. It's almost as though Tanya were being piggy-backed across the landscape instead of making her own way. Is there something I have overlooked?

Des: Individualization is being served of course, because Tanya's life experiences are uniquely different from those of any other human being. Don't forget that as Tanya continues to move further from the heavy vibrations of physical she relives, and takes constantly changing lessons from every moment spent with every host who piggy-backs her during the process of communication. Because of her many piggy-back journeys, she absorbs learning experiences and their many insights in a way that is quite removed from anything recognizable to the host, or to anyone else with direct experience of the physical.

Yes, she will miss out on many shades of physicality, including the exploration of possible futures, at least in terms we have discussed. In compensation she will immerse herself in the infinite dimensions of sensitivity, love, compassion, and the many emotions unknown to physical life; and take from them what her uniqueness and state of development make possible. Such emotional profoundness would make her unsurvivable if experienced directly in the realms of the negative energy of the physical. Tanya's spectrum of experiences in spirit is absorbed into her eternal soul, in order to complete the intricate patterns being sought. Her spiritual journey benefits her as ninety years in physical would not.

Q: During our discussions over the years, you and I have talked about Tanya. You said Miss Eleven occasionally was cheeky or angry or moody. I don't understand. You have explained that once removed from heavy vibrations, a spirit loses touch with negative energy. She no longer needs to be afflicted by it and express it. In Tanya's case, she died before being born, and probably never had the opportunity to encounter real negativity. So why and how did she get angry?

Des: Yes, at the time it puzzled me as well, although I can't remember what explanation my guidance offered. In communicating with me, Miss Eleven entered the realm of intensely heavy vibrations. This brought to the surface of her mind some of the negative emotions she experienced when last in physical form. Although Tanya was being guided and protected, nothing could change the fact that she was a child. She told it like it was. She didn't hide her emotions and was profoundly sensitive. Because of these factors, the youngster and I were learning lessons that were priceless to us both. Even then she was part of the conduit.

Our discussions continued almost daily for seven months, progressively moving her closer to my emotional proximity. Our past relationships in physical always were marked by either an intense closeness or intense dislike. Like magnets we attracted or repelled each other. The closer Miss Eleven came to me, to my physical energy, the more this influence played itself out.

Daughter's anger, mild by physical standards, was of no significance. Doubtless the interaction was foreseen by those responsible. What was significant was our uncommon ability to mesh positively at the physical level. This enabled a very effective dialogue, representing an important part of the framework of concepts that was being built within my mind.

Q: It's hard to imagine any spirit willingly moving into the physical without being dragged kicking and screaming. Even in Tanya's case, although she never remained in physical, she moved from a high level of spirit down to a very low level, via the physical.

Des: In spirit, but more especially in its higher reaches, it is recognized that the creative empowerment available in physical represents an unparalleled opportunity and privilege. Every second spent on the physical plane is seen as precious. A spirit clothed in flesh spends a few heartbeats in that environment, and as a consequence can change into a superior life form. Nothing is more important.

It should be remembered that in the normal course of events a physical journey includes the time spent after death in reliving, time after time, every significant event of that lifetime. Possible futures represent part of the physical journey, as do the growth opportunities offered by the sharing of life experiences in spirit among group members when they communicate.

Leaving the Physical Body

Q: Dying and detaching from the physical is a process going on for some time after the physical vehicle has broken down. Can you tell me more?

Des: The process can begin years before the body dies, especially in the case of an elderly person. It is not uncommon, as the years take their toll, for a person to become disinterested, to lose an appetite for the affairs of the physical. The body has served its purpose and is seen as offering little more. At one level or another, the individual is gently moving into the transition. The mind and the body cooperate in an orderly manner. Emotionally there is little stress.

    A possible exception involves medical intervention, when a patient is brought back, often at the urging of family members. When this happens the patient can be called on to die time and again before obtaining relief and release.

Reincarnation

Q: I thought a life in the physical world was necessary because of bad karma gathered during a previous life. This string of lives is supposed to continue until no more bad karma exists. Then we are free from suffering caused by the cycle of birth and death.

Des: The concept of reincarnation teaches a basic lesson relating to life on the physical plane in a way many people can understand. We are rewarded individually and collectively for doing what is positive and undergo discomfort or even pain for doing what is negative. Reincarnation is only one philosophy teaching this lesson. Different cultures and religions make use of their own exclusive analogies, parables and symbols, developed according to the needs of their followers. It all goes to develop human potential, and to foster individualization. This could be referred to as the evolvement of consciousness.

Science

Q: The theories you want to make known seem pretty far removed from every area of science and philosophy that I've come across.

Des: I think it is fair to suggest that science continues to evolve, and in the process rejects its own theories as they change. They are true for a certain amount of time and then become untrue. For example, in the early years of the nineteenth century it was proclaimed in scientific circles that never would it be possible, never in the course of human history, for a person to reach the speed of one hundred miles an hour. Although I must admit that I have seen slightly different figures and dates given in different accounts. To reach one hundred miles an hour, it was declared, invariably would crush the cardio-vascular system and cause death.

It was believed by the scientific establishment, after many research projects, that when meat decomposed it turned into maggots and then flies. The theory of a cycle of life was built along these lines. These theories now are discounted. They are no longer true.

It is logical to believe that present day theories will become untrue and replaced by others, and so on through the centuries.

So far as philosophical premises are concerned, I know so little that I am unable to comment. But then the message in this book is not mine.

Suicide

Q: A family member committed suicide recently. After talking to a minister I am fearful about his present situation. Can you put my mind at rest?

Des: I can tell you only what I believe. After his death, your family member is likely to remain in the same emotional space he occupied before his death. His suicide has resolved nothing. No longer is he able to resolve the issues which caused the trauma, so in the meantime he will remain trapped.

Having said that, without exception, a suicide victim will gravitate away from his misery as he loosens his attachment to the physical, and as the focus of his awareness shifts in the direction of group members seeking to reach him and provide consolation and understanding. Later he will join them. At that point he will feel a dawning sense of serenity and peace.

However, he will still have to face the fact that every second he avoided in physical as the result of his suicide, is a unique growth experience he has lost forever. But even that will be reconciled, as indeed every activity in physical is reconciled.

Q. The point has been made that there is no accident or coincidence. How does that relate to the suicide?

Des: There is no time. Once the suicide has taken place, it always was going to take place. The event is part of that individual's personal journey. It has always been intended, made inevitable by the victim's free will. Personally I find this explanation rather superficial and unconvincing. Nevertheless it is the best available to the analogy involved. The trauma can be influenced by the group in spirit whose members try to reach the suicidal person to provide focused strength and guidance. Sometimes this can sway the outcome, effectively providing a different future.

Q: What is the situation if the suicide victim believed his action will condemn him to hell? Does he not create that reality out of consciousness? Will he not end up in hell?

Des: Yes. Immediately after death, while still feeling his misery, he will occupy the state of hell his expectation has created within his mind. That is where he will languish until gravitating towards his group in spirit, and then joining them.

Hell is an extreme example of the earthbound state, which is a mental/emotional place of one's own making through which every person passes after separating from the physical, even evolved personalities moving back to spirit.

Although the suicide victim's action is regretted deeply, there is another brushstroke to the picture. Suicide is part of negative polarization. It does skew the individual's spiritual growth. It is a burden on both the group in spirit, and those left behind in physical. But it is a growth experience which represents a strand within the rich fabric of the world of heavy matter. It is part of the suffering we are here to contend with and to rise above eventually.

Q: Does suicide have a positive face?
Des: Yes and no. Yes, surprisingly, even if that face does carry only the shadow of a smile. If a person in physical places himself in such a harsh emotional environment, directly and indirectly, that he must fight for survival against overwhelming odds, it is a comment on the determination and strength of his spirit vehicle, even if he has misjudged his coping abilities.

No, if the person finds himself in his suicidal predicament because of self-indulgence.

Polarization and Negative Energy

Q: You were told by Val that you have dark energy around you, but we have been told almost nothing about dark energy.
Des: Dark energy is the accumulation of life experiences in environments that tend to be fraught with negativity. At some level this is retained as a program, a potential or predisposition, even if it is never acted upon.

Much of this will come from past lives and often is gender-sensitive. The female's nurturing and more selfless role throughout history leads her into more benign emotional situations. She becomes imprinted with them and the cycles they create. She is more gentle. There is little or no darkness.

On the other hand, the male always has been more focused on personal and group empowerment and the organizing of these resources. He may sacrifice his life for a cause, even if he doesn't understand. The female is far too pragmatic for that. In primal terms, if she dies her baby dies.

Throughout history the male is the one who is apt to protect his own people by contributing to the slaughter of others. He is capable of carrying out atrocities for a noble cause. Driven by these cycles of polarizing maleness he may function as a magnificent soldier but a miserable human being. All this will create darkness within him.

In the physical there are no whole human beings! The male and female is each really half a person. Driven by their differences, they need each other even as they are apt to repel each other. Polarization demands nothing less. In spirit, because every personality comprises male and female energy, the two aspects come together to form a more balanced completeness, a whole human being. There is no need for conflict, negativity and polarization.

In physical we learn because of the power of polarization. In spirit we learn because of its absence.

While a dominance of male personalities through a parade of past lives provides dark energy, it also provides a male's preoccupation with idealistic and philosophical concerns necessary for the continued advancement of the species. The presence of female past lives injects love and caring into that soul, and in the process dissolves dark energy. However something of the darkness remains as an acknowledgment, almost a signature, of the total journey. This will remain even in the Completed Being, as part of that which makes every human different from every other.

Sex in Spirit

Q: Is there an awareness of sex in spirit?

Des: Let's look at the physical first. It is normal for sex to be a reinforcing and initiating part of love. In physical, love is when we have our personal needs met. Sex is a part of that. Another part is primal. Let's put the two parts together. The parent loves the child. In that situation a mother's need to nurture comes to the fore, as does the father's need to protect. The child awakens both. The parents' personal needs are met.

Within the family environment we encounter the personal need to be included, to have a family identity, to be respected and to receive love and appreciation. In the mother's case she has a powerful need to feel secure, because an insecure environment places her children at risk. We need roots. We need to belong. Sex simply is a narrow and focused part of that love infrastructure. We are herd animals.

A student said to me once, "I don't agree that love is when we have our needs met. I love Jesus, and that emotion is selfless and giving."

My response was, "We all build our own truth within us. Yours is neither right nor wrong. It is yours. Mine is mine. All I'm doing is offering my truth for your consideration. I think you have a need for Jesus in your life, a valid and understandable need for something beyond the physical, something beyond yourself. This you identify as Jesus, therefore you embrace him. I celebrate the fact you have a beautiful way of meeting your emotional and intellectual needs."

Sex, however, can represent a blind, self-indulgent appetite, because every activity, emotion and thought in physical must defer to the process of polarization.

But in spirit-proper, as opposed to the earthbound state, negative energy is not present and so polarization is not present, especially in its higher reaches. There exists instead a compelling spiritual outpouring that is centered on self-love, an unfolding awareness that embraces everyone in the environment. Because the spirit loves self, the emotion gains expression by being directed to those who share the environment. Sex is not part of that because a physical presence is not a part of that. Something infinitely more significant and precious is available.

Sometimes when a young adult dies, a strong sexual awareness will remain as in physical, until the person grows away from all physical preoccupations. But if an individual has been fixated on sex, addicted to it, he will carry that imbalance into the after death state before gravitating away as he moves into spirit proper, significantly, retaining the particular lessons the experience offers.

Skeptics

Q: Are you open to our challenge to prove what it is you are claiming? In the modern world it is reasonable to ask for proof. We are doing so now.

Des: While inferring that scientific proof is the only way fact can be separated from fiction, skeptics tend to fall into the same trap as many others. They defer to one emotional need or another, and embrace a belief structure which comes closest to supporting and validating that need. They reach out for facts which give credibility to their beliefs, and reject facts which deny it. There is nothing wrong with this, because it is part of human nature. It leads the believer into a comfort zone which is relatively free from conflict. We all like comfort. Undeniably it is comforting to be convinced you are right, the other person is wrong, and there is only one truth. To use scientific facts as an absolute authority to prove you are right is a convenience.

A difference between the typical skeptic and the views expressed in this book is that the authors encourage respect and support for those holding different opinions. Indeed the idea is to empower others and celebrate the difference of opinion. There is no need to be defensive, elitist and territorial.

Perhaps there are different ways to be blindly skeptical, to embrace a viewpoint which meets emotional needs above all else. The scientific skeptic is not alone in surrendering to the power of emotional needs. Many religions appear to do so. "Our faith is the only true faith. Our God is the only true God. We are right and all others are wrong," is a cry which has hung over many communities and battlefields throughout history. People who believe in communicating with those who have died are as capable as anyone else of believing blindly what they want to believe.

None of this is surprising. It reflects the state of the human condition. It's where we are right now. We can't be where we are not.

Evolved Beings

Q: The picture that is drawn of an evolved individual in spirit fascinates me. We seem to be talking about an almost god-like life form, a Being of Light who transcends humanity. Can you help me to understand?

Des: The point has to be made that there are a vast number of different levels of evolvement. It's like the physical. Here there are many degrees and types of maturity, and ways in which maturity varies from one environment to another. The same is essentially the case in spirit. The people who exercise collective guidance within the total Human Organism comprise a small number of individuals who are more evolved than others. They are the parents within the human family.

On one occasion an overview of the human family was offered to me defining the relationship between the most and least mature members. It went like this:

Imagine a crowd of people making their way across a vast landscape. They walk huddled together. Leading them are the most mature individuals, their leaders, and trailing behind the others are the least mature. The journey is one of spiritual growth. They trudge for ten thousand kilometers before reaching their destination.

The distance between the first person and the last is seventy-five meters, completely insignificant compared with the vast distance to be covered. In terms of growth, the distance between "A" and the most primitive member of the race is tiny when measured against the total journey to be undertaken by the species.

It follows that, as the crowd pushes forward, Most Primitive Member soon will stand on the spot occupied by "A" a short time before, and then will move past it. "A" will remain just as far in the lead, or will have pulled further away from the group. This very simplistic word picture answers a number of questions.

The End Game

Q: In the physical world, which you say has been ordered up by the perfection of natural law, exactly what positive role does the sadistic killer play? Or the rapist or child torturer?

Des: A fundamental purpose of physicality is the presence of negative energy, itself a process creating negative cycles. One can become entrapped within this vortex.

Before birth a soul with particular lessons to learn finds certain inclinations and tendencies, coming from past lives, emerging as it moves further into the proximity of coarse physical matter. These subsequently are given a focus, because of the parents it has chosen and in turn, its upbringing. This will empower its emerging negative appetites as intended.

Q: How does the soul and the spirit associated with this particular life stand to benefit by calculatedly descending into depravity?

Des: Let's accompany the personality as he moves back into spirit following his death. After shedding his coarsest vibrations, he explores his past physical activities in great detail. By now stripped of the self-serving excuses he once used to justify his behavior, he is naked. He is immersed in the suffering of his victims.

This is possible in an environment largely devoid of negative energy for four reasons:

(1) Because of his activities in physical, by definition he carries relatively gross and coarse vibrations even in spirit.

(2) In returning to physical to explore his past circumstances, he further coarsens these vibrations.

(3) The relative sensitivity of every spirit vehicle makes it profoundly receptive to all emotions.

(4) Every person contains a unique web of natural law, which in this case hones and steers the extreme discomfort so the lessons offered are discerned and identified in the most effective manner.

Q: Why does the spirit choose to do such things to itself?

Des: Let's not forget that when we enter the physical plane, we come face to face with the inescapable negative energy which is a necessary part of physicality. This brings to the surface the desires we carry from past lives. They are presented so we may face them and overcome them, or alternatively become sucked further into their vortex, before we are able to overcome them. Either way we process them and their consequences during the period in spirit following that physical life.

Q: What happens then?

Des: As we continue to switch from spirit to physical and back again, we cast off what could be called the opposite of love, erasing its stain from our eternal soul. What remains are the beautiful qualities which the negative episodes have unfolded, the spiritual gems actually created by the harsh interfaces of material form.

Qualities such as forgiveness of self and others, the reluctance to judge another person, but rather to understand and to support, a willingness to guide, nurture and accept responsibility where this is appropriate, and the ability to give love as an unconditional measure of what we are. Because we have been to those dark places, we are able to feel for others who are still there.

We have discussed how emotions represent a continuum, with the negative at one end and the positive at the other. Once a particular negative emotion is given birth, developed and shaped by physical experience, its opposite positive emotion also is given birth within us so that subsequently it can be developed and shaped. This is one reason for the polarizing influences of material form. Eventually the negative is worked through leaving only the positive. Evolvement is the accumulation of an increasing field of positive emotions, and the awareness and enablement that natural law provides as a consequence.

Q: What about the victim of this person's brutality in physical?

Des: The victim came to physical in search of the very experiences he encountered. He has committed similar episodes of brutality in a past life, possibly involving the same person. He is seeking to cleanse himself, purge himself, develop new areas of understanding, and use the opportunities presented by the negative energy available in physical.

Q: Way back in a person's first past life, when no bad karma existed, how did the whole ghastly cycle kick in?

Des: Natural law is perfect, not ghastly. Negative energy in physical stirs primitive appetites that are an inherent part of human nature, such as self-indulgence, anger, jealousy and resentment. This is directed towards other people. Conflict is inevitable. Cycles become established. This has always been the case. There are as many ways for karmic cycles to be set up as there are different emotions available to the soul, as it uses and eventually rises above the negative energy. Precisely how this is done is a tool in the hands of the law of individuality.

It can be seen how the entire Human Organism comes together on the material plane to turn self-indulgence into selflessness, to unfold individuality, turn hatred or indifference to others' suffering into love, and to progress humanity from one level of evolvement to another. All is set in motion on the physical plane. All is centered on the presence of negative energy. A process which starts at the individual level and affects every person in physical, flows through to the total Organism and contributes to its ongoing creation.

Q: Is perfect justice served up to every single member of the human race regardless of circumstances?

Des: Yes. We have all immersed ourselves in negative activities in one life or another. We grow through such experiences, even as a small child grows with the activities of every day into an older child, then a young adult and finally a mature personality. Apparently there is no other way of growing.

Q: So if we do not stoop to brutality or evil at some time, we do not grow and mature spiritually? Perhaps a goodie-goodie two-shoes will end up spiritually stunted?

Des: We are talking about human beings here, not some imaginary species. We are talking about natural laws relating to human beings. It is inescapable that primitive behavior will be drawn from us during our first past life, in order that growth may flow in an orderly manner and that individualization may flower. Every baby is primitive in the way it expresses its needs! A parent would not call Baby brutal or evil. Growth is growth. There is nothing wrong with this. Serial past lives build within us self-acceptance, self-love and self-forgiveness so we can export these qualities to others in the external environment.

Think of an evolved personality. She is in the forefront, guiding the human family. She has already made her mistakes, learned from them and moved on. She is like the wise parent. She has grown through her childhood and adolescent immaturities, benefited from them, and accepted the responsibility of teaching others.

Q: An interesting question does present itself. Is there any way of growing spiritually that does not involve negative behavior?

Des: I am told the answer is yes. However the details fall outside the agenda of the conduit.

Q: Can you give me an example of this growing by the process of trial and error that is taking place right now, and which involves the entire Organism?

Des: Yes. Are we not indulging ourselves on the bounty of the land, squandering in the process, throwing away what we can't use, while twenty percent of the world's population is dying in misery because we use their share of the resources? The results of such behavior influence the entire Organism.

Q: Is the perfection of natural law not up to the task of remedying the situation?

Des: Oh yes.

Q: If your friend "A" wants to interest the unwashed masses on the material plane, why doesn't he organize a miracle or three? Even Uri Geller's alleged spoon-bending attracted widespread attention.

Des: I think it's the washed and well-dressed masses he is more interested in reaching. The physical is where a miracle happens in every life in every moment. This is where we create, where we turn one life-form into another as inescapably we grow by encountering experience after experience. Every thought, emotion, physical sensation, action, reaction and flight of fancy unfolds something within us that has never existed in the universe. It becomes ours forever. We have earned it. But it is up to us to take advantage of his advice.

Q: Do you have any opinion or evaluation on the information provided by the conduit?

Des: The information also speaks for me. In the developed world we have reached the point where we can be expected to accept responsibility for the physical environment and the wellbeing of our fellow travelers. We now possess the necessary awareness, the means and the opportunity. Only we can do it.

In nature every action has a reaction. If we jump off a high place we may get hurt. If we burn down the house there will be nowhere to live. If we poison the well we will have to dig another or have no water. If we fail to look after our health we may get sick. We must live with what we do or fail to do.

If a seed falls onto a dry rocky place, it will probably die. This is not right or wrong. It is natural law. The same principle applies to every human being, and to human beings collectively. Because we are a complex life form with free will we are tied into complex trains of cause and effect. We have always been given more latitude, the opportunity to make repeated mistakes and learn a little from each. We have always been nurtured and guided.

This has changed almost abruptly. From this point on more is expected of us because we are capable of delivering more. We are capable of accepting the baton of stewardship. The planet has become our responsibility. We have sufficient time and means to do what is necessary. We need only to redirect our free will to make it happen. Nobody can do this for us.

The details provided by the conduit offer slightly different things to different readers, depending on their needs and circumstances. The reader is free to take what he or she can relate to from these pages. For example, no longer is there any need to fear death and the threat of hell and damnation, which are ingrained in large sections of Christianity. Instead of being good out of dread we can embrace physical life as a privilege and an opportunity, being aware that we create ourselves with every thought, emotion and activity. Love and giving, as well as forgiveness, compassion and tolerance produce their own payback, because we are all part of a single body. By helping another we are helping ourselves.

Discrimination, religious conflict and elitism can be seen for what they are, namely a lack of any real commitment to understand the human condition and act on this understanding. Indifference to the plight of others reflects our self-indulgence.

All this notwithstanding, everything I do, I do for me, because every person, life form and object that is not me, merely is a thing in my environment that is there to create an aspect of me as I interact with it. In our universe there is only me and that which is not me. What is not me exists to create within me what otherwise would not be created.

At the same time we are all one! The foregoing sounds like a contradiction because an analogy is only an analogy. Examine its different parts in isolation.

Evaluate what we have put forward and be guided by your conscience and your free will. With the means available we have made a case. It is adequate. Please do with it what you will. The responsibilities, along with the consequences are yours to own.

Q: As part of the Christian community in a Christian country, I suggest that you are the one who has just poisoned the well.

Des: I disagree. The people sending this message have just dug an additional one, which you are all welcome to use because nobody owns it.

Epilogue

The following question was given to me during an assessment of the manuscript.

Q: You have a personal story to tell along with the revelations you obtained from spirit by means of the neuropsychological techniques in which you specialize. You were emotionally crippled by a fear of rejection because of trauma suffered as a young child. That experience was reinforced constantly during much of your marriage to the only person you allowed past your defenses. The rejection was continued during the weeks following her death. You seem to have a unique, certainly an uncommon, relationship with your wife. How is this story continuing to play itself out?

Des: During the months following her death, my awareness of rejection was overshadowed by three specters which never were far away.

The first involved the fact that, during my visits to Emmerson House, Val frequently begged me to take her home. Never before had I heard such desperate pleading, hoarsely squeezed out with whatever strength she had left. On every occasion I refused, year after year. Invariably she broke down in tears. Much of the time for three years she wept. All Val wanted was to come home to die, although she could not have survived outside the intensive-care environment.

The second was a question concerning the young grandchildren. What would I have felt in Val's predicament, knowing that the little guys rarely were allowed to glimpse me because my pitiful appearance might frighten or traumatize them? For the rest of their lives, was that how they would remember me? With a shudder?

The third question. Did the spirit within Val lead her to self-medicate, and destroy herself with a series of strokes, in order to make her available more quickly for work with the conduit? If so, this is a stark reminder of my own responsibilities to the conduit!

For a long time I have been aware that it is what we don't know which makes us feel sad, guilty, oppressed, or rejected. Now I know exactly what that means. I know that there is a spiritual reason for everything. At the emotional level I am complete, knowing with an absolute certainty that Val's peace and acceptance extend to include me in her environment. Emmerson House was just a snapshot in time, along with the other testing experiences in physical. They were necessary, but they have come and gone. Now I can get on with my life. I am free.

Acknowledgements

Perhaps not every postman is put in the position of acknowledging the people who have contributed to the letters he delivers. Anyway, that's me. I am the postman. What appears in the book was given to me to deliver.

First I would like to thank the friends who went through the manuscript and made constructive and commonsense suggestions on the manner in which I presented the information. These include Dolly Young, Tracy Metin, Michael Bannert, Monika Bannert, Adrienne Whitehouse, Cassandra Grove, Wendy Bryant, Gina Aburn and Sheryn McMurray.

I am grateful to Theo, a most talented young man who gave freely of his time and artistic excellence to create a visually stunning and captivating cover design. Although he resides at the other end of the world it was no coincidence that brought him to the project.

I would like to acknowledge Dr. Francine Shapiro who founded the famous neuropsychological modality Eye Movement Desensitization and Reprocessing (EMDR). On that bedrock a closely allied technique called Induced After

Death Communication (IADC) was developed by Dr. Allan L. Botkin. Without their contributions this book would not have been written. I was able to simplify both EMDR and IADC and turn them into a self-help modality that was used to channel the information appearing in The Littlest Crusade.

Also I must acknowledge my clients and students, some of whom became friends, who provided me over the years the clinical experience with my personal delivery mechanism for EMDR and IADC.

Finally I thank my family for the help and support which can be found only in a family. I'm not sure whether to thank my deceased wife Val or ask her to thank me. In any event we are a team, which in turn is part of something very much larger. To that extent we are both profoundly privileged.

About the Author

As a neurotherapist specializing in trance work, Desmond Long spent two years researching and using a breakthrough technique developed in stages by Francine Shapiro Ph.D and Alan L. Botkin, Psy.D, two eminent American mental healthcare professionals. Their efforts made possible a scientifically established but sketchy contact with people in the after-death state.

Desmond modified and enhanced these techniques to enable them to be used by a person on him or herself. There was a reason for this. From the time he was a young child he possessed the clairaudient (psychic) ability to communicate with deceased individuals. This was evolved over the years until he could enter into comprehensive exchanges of information.

When his wife died in 2007 he merged the scientific technique with his psychic gift and joined her. He was in for a shock! His visits were variously appalling and beautiful and enlightening as he met up with those in her environment every few days for nine months, exploring in intricate detail the secrets of the human condition that abruptly became available.

www.ingramcontent.com/pod-product-compliance
Lightning Source LLC
LaVergne TN
LVHW051827080426
835512LV00018B/2755